The Essential Guide
RESEARCH WRITING
ACROSS THE DISCIPLINES

Sixth Edition

James D. Lester

James Lester, Jr.
Austin Peay State University

PEARSON

Boston Columbus Indianapolis New York San Francisco Upper Saddle River
Amsterdam Cape Town Dubai London Madrid Milan Munich Paris Montreal Toronto
Delhi Mexico City São Paulo Sydney Hong Kong Seoul Singapore Taipei Tokyo

Senior Sponsoring Editor: Katharine Glynn
Senior Marketing Manager: Tom DeMarco
Production Manager: Ellen MacElree
Project Coordination, Editorial Services, and Text Design: Electronic
Publishing Services Inc., NYC
Art Rendering and Electronic Page Makeup: Jouve
Cover Designer/Manager: Wendy Ann Fredericks
Cover Art: © Shutterstock.com
Senior Manufacturing Buyer: Dennis J. Para
Printer and Binder: R. R. Donnelley and Sons Company—Crawfordsville
Cover Printer: Lehigh-Phoenix Color/Hagerstown

This title is restricted to sales and distribution in North America only.

For permission to use copyrighted material, grateful acknowledgment is
made to the copyright holders on p. 213, which are hereby made part of
this copyright page.

Library of Congress Cataloging-in-Publication Data

Lester, James D., (date).
    The essential guide: research writing across the disciplines /
James D. Lester, James D. Lester, Jr. — 6th ed.
        p. cm.
    Includes bibliographical references and index.
    ISBN 978-0-321-85343-1 (student ed.) — ISBN-10: 0-321-85343-1
1.   Report writing—Handbooks, manuals, etc.
2.   Research—Handbooks, manuals, etc. I.   Lester, James D.,
(date) II.   Title.
    LB2369.L39 2012
    808'.02—dc23

                                                    2012024728

Copyright © 2013, 2011, and 2008 by Pearson Education, Inc.

4 5 6 7 8 9 10—DOC—15 14

www.pearsonhighered.com
Student Edition: ISBN-13: 978-0-321-85343-1
ISBN-10: 0-321-85343-1

Brief Contents

Detailed Contents

Preface

This sixth edition of *The Essential Guide: Research Writing Across the Disciplines* provides several indispensable features for students and instructors in first-year composition courses as well as upper-level researchers, including:

- **Low cost, small trim size, and concise coverage** make this research guide a valuable but non-intrusive supplement to a core text or anthology in any college course that requires a research paper.

- **Non-intimidating, step-by-step instructions on all aspects of the research process** help students through this daunting task.

- **Coverage of Internet sources** includes attention to critical evaluation of these sources and tips for using discipline-specialized search engines.

- **Strategies for developing an argument in a research paper** are presented, as are organizational paradigms for other common types of research papers.

- **Chapter on preparing electronic projects explains methods** for incorporating slide presentations, web sites, web pages, and digital graphics into the research paper.

What's New in the Sixth Edition?

- **New "Clear Target" sections** at the beginning of each chapter provide learning objectives that serve as a ready guide to help students find documentation information quickly and to chart the direction of their research project.

- **Chapters 3 and 6 now include new explanations of online research techniques** using social media, such as blogs and wikis as well as keyword searches with expanded Boolean operators, to ensure that students can utilize cutting-edge research tools and strategies.

- **Chapter 14 includes new guidelines for presenting electronic research projects** including expanded explanations for using graphics and preparing a writing portfolio.

- **More than 100 new examples of documentation** styles are given in Chapters 10 to 13.

- **Updated coverage of online research strategies in Chapter 3** shows students where to find the most pertinent Internet search engines including detailed advice on where to find respected scholarly sources.

- **Expanded coverage of plagiarism and unintentional plagiarism** provides useful guidance to help students avoid plagiarism problems.

- **Updated coverage about using databases in Chapter 2 provides** accurate and useful search information to help students go beyond general Internet search results to locate credible, authoritative sources.

Online and Field Resources for Research

Chapter 2 explains how to use a library's online resources. It spotlights the academic databases that can be accessed through the library's electronic system. Chapter 3 encourages controlled Internet searches but sets guidelines for acceptable academic sites. The text provides students with a comprehensive list, by discipline, of important search engines. In Chapter 4, the coverage of field research helps students conduct interviews, questionnaires, and correspondence by e-mail and web conferencing.

An Emphasis on Academic Integrity

Electronic retrieval has made plagiarism an all too common problem. Chapter 5 explains what constitutes plagiarism and shows students that both intended and unintended plagiarism are serious violations of academic conduct.

Focus on Critical Reading

Chapters 6 and Chapter 7 give valuable pointers on such matters as identifying the best sources, evaluating them for relevancy, authority, and accuracy, and—just as important—creating notes that summarize, quote, and paraphrase effectively and to a point. This section shows students how to use their notes to build an annotated bibliography and a review of the literature on a narrowed topic.

Composing with Sources

The Essential Guide helps students find reliable sources, create effective notes in a variety of fashions, and then—most important of all—blend those sources into an effective piece of writing, one in which the student's voice is not lost yet the sources provide support and confirmation of key theories. Thus, Chapters 8 and 9 on blending sources for an academic style are ones that instructors not only assign but walk with the students through the material.

Writing in the Disciplines

The default style for textual instruction in the text is the MLA style for students and instructors in literature and composition, as promoted in the first ten chapters of the book. However, the book also explores research style through the lenses of other disciplines in the social sciences, natural sciences, applied sciences, and humanities.

Style examples as well as student papers throughout the book show students the most up-to-date models and citation formats. Hence, science students can examine and test a hypothesis while literature students build upon a thesis statement. Science students do more field research than students in philosophy or history. In addition, science students do different things with their testing and their comments on the results. Thus, several aspects of academic writing are examined and explained in this book—the footnote system, the name and year system, and the citation-sequence system.

Electronic Presentations

The Essential Guide includes a chapter (Chapter 14) for students who wish to present their research project electronically. The chapter explains the various methods for developing the research paper with slide presentations, web pages, websites, and digital graphics. It also explains the methods for delivering the paper by e-mail, CD-ROM, and website.

Keeping Current to the Latest Standards

This sixth edition of *The Essential Guide: Research Writing Across the Disciplines* has been updated to conform to these basic style guides:

- *Chicago Manual of Style*, 16th edition, 2010
- *MLA Handbook for Writers of Research Papers*, 7th edition, 2009
- *Publication Manual of the American Psychological Association*, 6th edition, 2010
- *Scientific Style and Format: The CSE Manual for Authors, Editors, and Publishers*, 7th edition, 2006

Student Papers

To demonstrate MLA style, the text contains three papers:

1. "Annotated Bibliography" by Norman Delgado
2. "Gender Communication: A Review of the Literature" by Kaci Holz
3. "Wilfred Owen—Battlefront Poet" by Anthony Murphy

To demonstrate APA style, the text features:

"More Academics for the Cost of Less Engaged Children" by Caitlin Kelley

To show the CMS footnote style, the text displays:

"Prehistoric Wars: We've Always Hated Each Other" by Jamie Johnston

To demonstrate the CSE number style, the text presents:

"Diabetes Management: A Delicate Balance" by Sarah E. Bemis

The Ancillary Package

The publication package includes these features:

- **E-mail access to the author.** The author is available to instructors and students to answer questions on style and format. You may contact the author at jlester5@charter.net or james.lester@cmcss.net.
- **MyCompLab®.** MyCompLab uniquely integrates proven resources and assessment tools with a student's own writing. This seamless and flexible application, built for writers by writers, helps instructors and students accomplish everyday composition tasks more easily and effectively.

Acknowledgments

The author wishes to thank those who have been instrumental in the development of *The Essential Guide: Research Writing Across the Disciplines*, 6th edition. For editorial assistance that kept me focused, special thanks are extended to Joe Opiela and Katharine Glynn. I am also grateful to the production team at Pearson and at EPS, especially Ellen MacElree and Jennifer Fricker. Finally, I want to recognize a great group of reviewers whose penetrating and perceptive suggestions have informed this edition: James Allen, College of DuPage; Doug Downs, Montana State University; Linda Eicken, Cape Fear Community College; Jennifer Penry Romano, Herzing University; Juliette Berning Schaefer, Ohio Dominican University.

Special thanks is extended to student authors Caitlin Kelley, Jamie Johnston, Norman Delgado, Kaci Holz, Anthony Murphy, and Sarah E. Bemis. Love and appreciation goes to my family, friends, and colleagues.

James D. Lester, Jr.
jlester5@charter.net
or
james.lester@cmcss.net

Writing from Research

Clear Targets

Communication begins when we make an initial choice to speak or to record our ideas in writing. This chapter charts a direction for your research project:

- Generating ideas and discovering a well-focused topic
- Exploring sources through critical reading
- Developing a thesis statement to direct your analysis of the topic

A piece of writing—whether it is a history paper, a field report, or a research project—commits our personal concerns to public knowledge. Many people can examine our written document and then make judgments about our beliefs. That scrutiny is intimidating.

Writing is an outlet for the inquisitive and creative nature in each of us. Our writing is affected by the richness of our language, by our background and experiences, by our targeted audience, and by the form of expression that we choose. With perceptive enthusiasm for relating detailed concepts and honest insights, we discover the power of our own words. The satisfaction of writing well and relating our understanding to others provides intellectual stimulation and insight into our own beliefs and values.

As a writer, you will find that your assignments extend past personal thoughts and ideas to explore more complex aspects of academic studies. This exploration will make you confident in your ability to find information and present it effectively in all kinds of ways and for various writing projects:

- A theme in a first-year composition course on the value of social media, web logs, and other online discussion groups
- A history paper on Herbert Hoover's ineffectual policies for coping with the Great Depression of the early 1930s
- A report for a physical fitness class on the benefits of ballroom dancing as exercise

- A sociological field report on free and reduced lunches for school-aged children
- A brief biographical study of a famous person, such as labor leader César Chávez

All of these papers require some type of "researched writing." Papers similar to these will appear on your schedule during the first few years of your college career and will increase in frequency in upper-division courses.

Each course of study and each instructor will make different demands on your talents, yet all will stipulate *researched writing*. Your research project will advance your theme and provide convincing proof for your inquiry.

- *Researched writing* grows from investigation.
- *Researched writing* establishes a clear purpose.
- *Researched writing* develops analysis for a variety of topics.

With the guidance of your instructor, you will make inquiry to advance your own knowledge as well as the data for future research by others.

1a Generating Ideas and Focusing the Subject

You can generate ideas for research and focus on the issues with a number of techniques.

- Relate your personal experiences to scholarly topics and academic disciplines.
- Speculate about the subject by listing issues, asking questions, engaging in free writing, talking with others, and using other idea-generating methods.
- Examine online sources.
- Read textbooks and reference books.

Relate Your Personal Ideas to a Scholarly Problem

Draw on yourself for ideas, keep a research journal, ask yourself questions, and get comfortable with new terminology. Contemplate personal issues to generate ideas worthy of investigation. At a quiet time, begin writing, questioning, and pushing on the various buttons of your mind for your feelings and attitudes. Your research paper should reflect your thinking in response to the sources. It should not merely report what others have said. If possible, combine a personal interest with one aspect of your academic studies:

PERSONAL INTEREST:	Skiing
ACADEMIC SUBJECT:	Sports Medicine
POSSIBLE TOPICS:	"Protecting the Knees"
	"Therapy for Strained Muscles"
	"Skin Treatments"

You might also consider social issues that affect you and your family:

PERSONAL INTEREST:	The behavior of my child in school
ACADEMIC SUBJECT:	Education
POSSIBLE TOPICS:	"Children Who Are Hyperactive"
	"Should School Children Take Medicine to Calm Their Hyperactivity?"

Your cultural background can prompt you toward detailed research into your roots, your culture, and the mythology and history of your ethnic background:

ACADEMIC SUBJECT:	History
ETHNIC BACKGROUND:	Hispanic
PERSONAL INTEREST:	Struggles of the Hispanic child in an American classroom
POSSIBLE TOPIC:	"Bicultural Experiences of Hispanic Students: The Failures and Triumphs"

Developing a Research Journal

Unlike a diary of personal thoughts about your daily activities or a journal of creative ideas, such as poems, stories, or scenarios, the **research journal** enables you to list issues, raise questions, create notes, and develop pieces of free writing. The research journal can be created in a handwritten notebook or as a document file on your personal computer.

You should build the journal primarily with **free writing** as well as **keywords and phrases** that come to mind. These establish primary categories for your research. One student listed several terms and phrases about the use of midwives in the rural Southeastern mountains:

natural childbirth	disinfectants	recovery time
prenatal care	medicines	delivery
hardships	complications	sterilization
delivery problems	deaths	cost

In her research journal she began writing notes on the various topics, such as this one:

> The cost of delivery by a midwife in the mother's home differs so greatly from the cost of a doctor and a hospital that we can only appreciate the plight of those using this procedure.

The research journal also provides a place for preliminary outlining to find the major and minor issues, as shown here:

Midwives in the Rural Southeast Mountains

Preparation:	Delivery:	Recovery:	Cost:
prenatal care	natural childbirth	after delivery	one fee
sterilization	medicines	recovery time	
disinfectants	delivery techniques	deaths	

Asking Questions

Asking questions in your research journal can focus your attention on primary issues, and your subsequent notes to answer the questions can launch your investigation. For example, having read Henry Thoreau's essay "Civil Disobedience," one writer posed these questions:

> What is "civil disobedience"?
> Is dissent legal? Is it moral? Is it patriotic?
> Is dissent a liberal activity? Conservative?
> Should the government encourage or stifle dissent?
> Is passive resistance effective?

Answering the questions can lead the writer to a central issue or argument, such as "Civil Disobedience: Shaping Our Nation."

Academic disciplines across the curriculum invite questions that might provoke a variety of answers and give focus to the subject, as with "sports gambling."

ECONOMICS:	Does sports gambling benefit a college's athletic budget? Does it benefit the national economy?
PSYCHOLOGY:	What is the effect of gambling on the mental attitude of the college athlete who knows that huge sums hang on the balance of his or her performance?

HISTORY:	Does gambling on sporting events have an identifiable tradition?
SOCIOLOGY:	What compulsion in human nature prompts people to gamble on athletic prowess?
POLITICAL SCIENCE:	What laws exist in this state for the control of illegal sports gambling? Are they enforced?

Using Key Terminology

Each discipline has its own terminology. For example, in research for a paper on retail marketing you might learn to refer to "the demographics" of a "target audience." In psychological research you might learn to use the phrases "control group" and "experimental group." One student found essential words for her paper on diabetes:

diabetes	diabetes mellitus	glucose
insulin	metabolize	hyperglycemia
pancreas	ketacidosis	ketones

She learned the meaning of each term and applied them properly in her paper, giving her work a scholarly edge.

Talking with Others to Find and Refine the Topic

Sometime early in your project, consult with others to get feedback on your possible topic and its issues. You can accomplish this task by personally interviewing appropriate people and participating in online discussion groups.

Personal Interviews

A personal interview, whether conducted face to face, by telephone, or by e-mail, allows you to consult with experts and people in your community for ideas and reactions to your subject. Explore a subject for key ideas while having coffee or a soda with a colleague, relative, or work associate.

HINT: Casual conversations that contribute to your understanding of the subject need not be documented. However, a formal interview or an in-depth discussion with an expert will demand credit in your text and a citation on the Works Cited page at the end of your paper.

Online Discussion Groups

What are other people saying about your subject? You might use the computer to share ideas and messages with other scholars interested in your subject. Somebody may answer a question or point to an interesting aspect which has not occurred to you. With discussion groups you have a choice:

- Classroom e-mail groups that participate in online discussions of various issues
- Online courses that feature a discussion room
- Real-time chatting and discussion groups with participants online at the same time, in some cases with audio and video

During an online chat conversation, you might find a few ideas on your topic; however, *heed this warning*: participants may use fictitious names, provide unreliable sources, and be highly opinionated in some instances, and therefore *they cannot be quoted in your paper*. The best you might gain is marginal insight into the ideas of people who are often eccentric and who hide behind their anonymity.

Using Online Searches to Refine a Topic

The Internet provides a quick and easy way to find a topic and to refine it to academic standards; however, do not neglect the library's academic databases and its electronic book catalog.

Using an Online Subject Directory

Articles on the Internet offer ideas about how other people approach the subject, and these ideas can help you refine your topic. Use the subject directory in a search engine, such as Google.com, to probe from a general topic to specific articles (Health > Diseases > Blood disorders > Anemia). Use a keyword search when you already have a specific topic. Thus, entering the word *anemia* will send you immediately to a variety of web articles. See Chapter 3, pages 36–51, for information about searching the Internet.

Utilizing Databases

Go to the reliable databases available through your library, such as Info Trac, PsychINFO, UMI ProQuest, or EBSCOhost. These are monitored Internet sites filtered by editorial boards and peer review. Many articles on these databases appeared first in print. In many cases you can read an abstract of the article before reading the full text. Look for a reputable sponsor, especially a university, museum, or professional organization. When you find a source, you can also print the article without going into the stacks.

Electronic Book Catalogs

Use your library's computerized index to find books, periodicals, DVD holdings, and similar items. Enter a keyword term or phrase, such as *Nancy Pelosi,* and you will get a listing of all relevant sources by and about the first woman speaker of the House. The book catalog will not index the titles to articles in magazines and journals, but it will tell you which periodicals are housed in the library and whether they are housed in a printed volume or in an electronic database (see immediately above). Instructors will want you to consult books during your research, so follow these steps:

1. Enter a keyword, such as *nutrition*, that will generate a reasonably sized list.
2. Examine the various entries in detail, starting with the most recent, to find books related to your topic.
3. In the stacks, find and examine each book for relevance. *Tip:* While in the stacks, examine nearby books, for they will likely treat the same subject.

Online and CD-ROM Encyclopedias

Browsing an online encyclopedia, such as Encyclopedia.com or Britannica Online Encyclopedia, can give you a good feel for the depth and strength of the subject and suggest a list of narrowed topics. You might also check with a librarian, a department office, and your instructor for CD-ROM discs and videos in a specialty area, such as mythology, poetry, or American history. These media forms often can be found in local bookstores or by purchase over the Internet.

Using Textbooks and Reference Books

Dipping into your own textbooks can reward you with topic ideas, and a trip to the library to examine books and indexes in the reference room also can be beneficial.

Library Books and Textbooks

With your working topic in hand, do some exploratory reading. Carefully examine the **titles** of books, noting key terminology. Search a book's **table of contents** for topics. A history book on the American Civil War might display these headings:

> The Clash of Amateur Armies
> Real Warfare Begins
> The Navies
> Confederate High-Water Mark

If any heading looks interesting to you, go to the book's **index** for additional headings, such as this sample:

Jefferson Davis, President of the Confederate States
   evacuates Richmond, 574, 576
   foreign relations, 250, 251
   imprisonment of, 567
   inauguration, 52–53
   peace proposals, 564–65

Perhaps the topic on peace proposals will spur an interest in all peace proposals; that is, how do nations end their wars and send the troops home safely?

Reference Books

If you do not have access to an electronic database, refer to printed indexes, such as the *Readers' Guide to Periodical Literature, Bibliographic Index,* and *Humanities Index.* Searching in reference books under a keyword or phrase usually leads to a list of critical articles on the subject.

HINT: Topic selection goes beyond choosing a general category (e.g., "single mothers"). It includes finding a research-provoking issue or question, such as "The foster parent program seems to have replaced the orphanage system. Has it been effective?" That is, you need to take a stand, adopt a belief, or begin asking questions. For more information, see Section 1d, "Drafting a Research Proposal."

1b Developing a Thesis, an Enthymeme, or a Hypothesis

One central statement will usually control an essay's direction and content, so as early as possible, begin thinking in terms of a controlling idea. Each type shown below has a separate mission:

- A **thesis statement** advances a conclusion that the writer will defend: *Contrary to what some philosophers have advanced, human beings have always participated in wars.*
- An **enthymeme** uses a *because* clause to make a claim the writer will defend: *There has never been a "noble savage," as such, because even prehistoric human beings fought frequent wars for numerous reasons.*

- A **hypothesis** is a theory that must be tested in the laboratory, in the literature, and/or by field research to prove its validity: *Human beings are motivated by biological instincts toward the physical overthrow of perceived enemies.*

Let us look at each type in more detail.

Thesis Statement

A thesis expands your topic into a scholarly proposal, one that you will try to prove and defend in your paper. It does not state the obvious, such as "Langston Hughes was a great poet from Harlem." That sentence cannot provoke an academic discussion because readers know that any published poet has talent. The writer must narrow and isolate one issue by finding a critical focus, such as this one:

Langston Hughes used a controversial vernacular language that paved the way for later artists, even today's rap musicians.

This statement advances an idea that the writer can develop fully and defend with evidence. The writer has made a connection between the subject, *Langston Hughes,* and the focusing agent, *vernacular language.* A general thesis might state:

Certain functional foods can prevent disease.

But note how your interest in an academic area can color the thesis:

BIOLOGICAL APPROACH:	Functional foods may be a promising addition to the diet of those wishing to avoid certain diseases.
ECONOMIC APPROACH:	Functional foods can become an economic weapon in the battle against rising health care costs.
HISTORIC APPROACH:	Other civilizations, including primitive tribes, have known about food's healing properties for centuries. Why did we let modern chemistry blind us to the benefits?

A thesis sets in motion the writer's examination of specific ideas the study will explore and defend. Thus, when confronted by a general topic, such as "television," adjust it to an academic interest, as with "Video replays have improved football officiating but slowed the game" or "Video technology has enhanced arthroscopic surgery."

Your thesis statement is not your conclusion or your answer to a problem. Rather, the thesis anticipates your conclusion by setting in motion the examination of facts and pointing the reader toward the special idea of your paper, which you will save for the conclusion.

Enthymeme

Your instructor might want the research paper to develop an argument as expressed as an enthymeme, which is a claim supported with a *because* clause. An enthymeme has a structure that depends on one or more unstated assumptions. Example:

> Hyperactive children need medication because ADHD is a medical disorder, not a behavioral problem.

The claim that children need medication is supported by the stated reason that the condition is a medical problem, not one of behavior. This writer will need to address the unstated assumption that medication alone will solve the problem.

> Participating in one of the martial arts, such as Tae Kwan Do, is good for children because it promotes self-discipline.

The claim that one organized sporting activity is good for children rests on the value of self-discipline. Unstated is the assumption that one sport, the martial arts, is good for children in other areas of development, such as physical conditioning. The writer might also address other issues, such as aggression or a combat mentality.

Hypothesis

A hypothesis proposes a theory or suggests an explanation for the purpose of argument or investigation. Here is an example:

> Discrimination against girls and young women in the classroom, known as "shortchanging," hinders the chances of women to develop their full academic potential.

This statement could produce a theoretical study if the student cites literature on the ways in which teachers "shortchange" students. A professional educator, on the other hand, would probably conduct extensive research in many classroom settings to defend the hypothesis with scientific observation.

Sometimes the hypothesis is *conditional:*

> Our campus has a higher crime rate than other state colleges.

This assertion on a conditional state of being could be tested by statistical comparison.

At other times the hypothesis will be *relational:*

> Class size affects the number of written assignments by writing instructors.

This type of hypothesis claims that as one variable changes, so does another, or that something is more or less than another.

It could be tested by examining and correlating class size and assignments.

At other times, the researcher will produce a *causal* hypothesis:

A child's choice of a toy is determined by television commercials.

This causal hypothesis assumes the mutual occurrence of two factors and asserts that one factor is responsible for the other. The student who is a parent could conduct research to prove or disprove the supposition.

Thus, your paper, motivated by a hypothesis, might be a theoretical examination of the literature, but it might also be an actual visit to an Indian burial ground or a field test of one species of hybrid corn. Everything is subject to examination, even the number of times you blink while reading this text. See also pages 52–60 for more information on field research.

C H E C K L I S T

Narrowing a General Subject into a Working Topic

Unlike a general subject, a focused topic should:

- Examine one significant issue, not a broad subject
- Argue from a thesis, enthymeme, or hypothesis
- Address a knowledgeable reader and carry that reader to another plateau of knowledge
- Have a serious purpose, one that demands analysis of the issues, argues from a position, and explains complex details
- Meet the expectations of the instructor and conform to the course requirements

---

1c   Using Your Thesis to Chart the Direction of Your Research

Often, the thesis statement will set the direction of the paper's development.

Arrangement by Issues

The thesis statement might force the writer to address various issues and positions.

THESIS:	Misunderstandings about organ dona-tion distort reality and set serious limits on the availability of those persons who need an eye, a liver, or a healthy heart.
ISSUE 1.	Many myths mislead people into believ-ing that donation is unethical.
ISSUE 2.	Some fear that as a patient they might be put down early.
ISSUE 3.	Religious views sometimes get in the way of donation.

This outline, though brief, provides three categories that require detailed research in support of the thesis. The note taking can be focused on these three issues.

Arrangement by Cause/Effect

In other cases, the thesis suggests development by cause/effect issues. Notice that the next writer's thesis on television's educational values points the way to four very different areas worthy of investigation.

THESIS:	Television can have positive effects on a child's language development.
CONSEQUENCE 1.	Television introduces new words.
CONSEQUENCE 2.	Television reinforces word usage and proper syntax.
CONSEQUENCE 3.	Literary classics come alive verbally on television.
CONSEQUENCE 4.	Television provides the subtle rhythms and musical effects of accomplished speakers.

The outline above can help the writer produce four positive con-sequences of television viewing.

Arrangement by Interpretation and Evaluation

Evaluation will evolve from thesis statements that judge a subject by a set of criteria, such as your analysis of a poem, movie, or museum display. Notice how the next student's thesis will require interpreta-tion of Hamlet's character.

THESIS:	Shakespeare manipulates the stage settings for Hamlet's soliloquies to uncover his unstable nature and forecast his failure.

1.   His soul is dark because of his mother's incest.
2.   He appears impotent in comparison with the actor.
3.   He is drawn by the magnetism of death.
4.   He realizes he cannot perform cruel, unnatural acts.
5.   He stands ashamed by his inactivity in comparison.

Arrangement by Comparison

Sometimes a thesis stipulates a comparison on the value of two sides of an issue, as shown in one student's preliminary outline:

THESIS: Discipline often involves punishment, but child abuse adds another element: the gratification of the adult.

COMPARISON 1:   A spanking has the interest of the child at heart, but a beating or a caning has no redeeming value.

COMPARISON 2:   Time-outs remind the child that relationships are important and to be cherished, but lock-outs in a closet only promote hysteria and fear.

COMPARISON 3:   The parent's ego and selfish interests often take precedence over the welfare of the child or children.

C H E C K L I S T

Evaluating Your Overall Plan

1. What is my thesis? Will my notes and records defend and illustrate my proposition? Is the evidence convincing?
2. Have I found the best plan for developing the thesis with elements of argument, evaluation, cause/effect, or comparison?
3. Should I use a combination of elements; that is, do I need to evaluate the subject, examine the causes and consequences, and then set out the argument?

1d   Drafting a Research Proposal

A research proposal helps to clarify and focus a research project. It comes in two forms: (1) a short paragraph to identify the project for approval of your instructor or (2) several pages to give background information, your rationale for conducting the study, a review of the literature, your methods, and the thesis, enthymeme, or hypothesis you plan to defend.

Writing a Short Research Proposal

A short proposal identifies five essential ingredients of your project:

- The specific topic
- The purpose of the paper (explain, analyze, argue)
- The intended audience (general or specialized)
- Your position as the writer (informer, evaluator, or advocate)
- The preliminary thesis statement or opening hypothesis

One writer developed this brief proposal:

The world is running out of fresh water while we sip our Evian. However, the bottled water craze signals something—we don't trust our fresh tap water. We have an emerging crisis on our hands, and some authorities forecast world wars over water rights. The issue of water touches almost every facet of our lives, from religious rituals and food supply to disease and political instability. We might frame this hypothesis: Water will soon replace oil as the economic resource most treasured by nations of the world. However, that assertion would prove difficult to defend and may not be true at all. Rather, we need to look elsewhere, at human behavior, and at human responsibility for preserving the environment for our children. Accordingly, this paper will examine (1) the issues with regard to supply and demand, (2) the political power struggles that may emerge, and (3) the ethical implications for those who control the world's scattered supply of fresh water.

Writing a Detailed Research Proposal

A long proposal presents specific details concerning the project. It has more depth and a greater length than the short proposal, as shown above. The long proposal should include some or all of the following elements:

1. *Cover page* with title of the project, your name, and the person or agency to whom you are submitting the proposal (see page 116 for details on writing titles and page 149 for the form of a title page).
2. An *abstract* that summarizes your project in 50 to 100 words (see page 168 for an example).
3. A *purpose statement* with your *rationale* for the project (see the short proposal above for an example). Use *explanation* to review and itemize factual data. One writer explained how diabetes can be managed (see Sarah E. Bemis's essay on pages 194–201). Use *analysis* to classify various parts of the subject and to investigate each one in depth (see Anthony Murphy's paper on poet Wilfred Owen, pages 150–154). Use *persuasion* to question the general attitudes about a problem and then to affirm new theories, advance a solution, recommend a course of action, or—at least—invite the reader into an intellectual dialogue (see Jamie Johnston's paper on prehistoric wars, pages 184–190).
4. A *statement of qualification* that explains your experience and perhaps the special qualities you bring to the project (i.e., you are the parent of a child with ADHD). If you have no experience with the subject, you can omit the statement of qualification.
5. A *review of the literature* that surveys the articles and books that you have examined in your preliminary work (see pages 100–108 for an explanation and an example of a review of literature).

1e Establishing a Schedule

The steps for producing a research paper have remained fundamental for many years. You will do well to follow them, even to the point of setting deadlines on the calendar for each step. In the spaces below, write dates to remind yourself when deadlines should be met.

_____ Finding and narrowing a topic. Your topic must have a built-in question or argument so that you can interpret an issue and cite the opinions found in the source materials.

_____ Drafting a thesis and research proposal. Even if you are not required to create a formal research proposal, you need to draft a plan to help direct and organize your research before you begin in-depth reading and research. See Section 1d.

_____ Creating notes. Begin entering notes in a digital or printed research journal. Some notes will be summaries, while others might be exact quotations or paraphrases of the original material. Chapter 8 details the techniques for effective note taking.

_____ Organizing and outlining. You may be required to create an organized, formal outline. Outlining and organizational models for your ideas are presented in Chapter 7.

_____ Drafting the paper. During your writing, let your instructor scan the draft to give you feedback and guidance. The instructor may also encourage peer reviews and classroom workshops and offer in-class review of your work in progress. See Chapter 9 for more details on drafting in an academic style.

_____ Formatting the paper. Proper document design places your paper within the required format for your discipline. Chapter 10–13 provide the guidelines for the various disciplines.

_____ Writing a list of your references. You will need to list the various sources used in your study. Chapter 10 provides documentation guidelines for MLA style.

_____ Revising and proofreading. Be conscientious about examining your manuscript and making final corrections. Chapter 9 gives you tips on formatting, revision, and editing.

_____ Submitting the manuscript. Like all writers, at some point you will need to "publish" your paper—on paper, through e-mail to your instructor, on a USB flash drive, to Blackboard or a similar site, or on your own web page.

2

Gathering Sources in the Library

Clear Targets

The library should be the center of your research, whether you access it electronically or visit in person. This chapter launches your research through scholarly publications:

- Utilizing the library's electronic resources catalog
- Exploring electronic databases and indexes
- Building your research journal

As the repository of the best books and periodicals, the articles that you access through the library are, in the main, written by scholars and published in journals and books only after careful review by a board of like-minded scholars.

2a   Launching the Library Search

In today's modern digital libraries, sources can be accessed just as easily as the Internet. In fact, most of the databases are part of the web. Logged in at the library, you can download articles to your computer, print files, and read some books online. Your initial strategy will normally include three stages: the initial search to gauge the academic atmosphere for your subject, fine-tuning your focus for in-depth searching, and building your own electronic journal with a working bibliography, printouts, and downloaded items. In addition, it will benefit you to stroll through your library to identify its various sections and make mental notes of the types of information available there.

Begin your initial search at the library's electronic book catalog and electronic databases because they will:

- Show the availability of source materials representing diverse opinions.
- Provide a beginning set of reference citations, abstracts, full-text articles, and books, some with full text for printing or downloading

- Help to restrict the subject and narrow your focus
- Give an overview of the subject by showing how others have discussed it

> **HINT:** Today's college library not only houses academic books and periodicals, it connects you by the Internet to thousands of academic resources that you cannot reach any other way. When you visit your college library in person or by computer link, you can be assured of getting sources that have been reviewed carefully and judged worthy of your time and interest. There is no assurance of sources' legitimacy when you use a general Internet search engine, which cannot access the scholarship at the academic sites. A general search engine, such as Google or Lycos, might send you anywhere. The library's databases will send you to reputable sources.

2b   Using the Library's Electronic Resources Catalog

Your library's computerized catalog probably has a special name, such as LIBNET, FELIX, ACORN, UTSEARCH, and so forth. It provides details on the various materials your library has available.

Books

The electronic book catalog lists every book in the library filed by subject, author, and title along with the call number, its location in the stacks, and its availability, as shown in this example:

> *Nutrition and Diet Therapy*
> Carroll A. Lutz and Karen Rutherford Przytulski, ed.
> Subjects: Nutrition research / Dietetics research
> Location: General Book Collection, Level 3
> Call number: WB 400 L975N 2011
> Status: Available

In many cases, clicking on the title will give you an abstract of the book. In some cases, the library's catalog will provide access to electronic books on the Internet, as shown by this example, which provides a URL hyperlink:

> *Nutrition in Early Life* [electronic resource]
> Edited by Jane B. Morgan and John W. T. Dickerson
> Internet access: http://www.library.tmc.edu

Journals

The electronic book catalog includes references to journals in bound volumes at the library or journals on the Internet, with links for accessing them.

> *Journal of Nutrition Education and Behavior*
> Availability: Periodicals Collection, Level 1
> This journal is available at the library.

> *The American Journal of Clinical Nutrition* [electronic resource]
> Internet access: Full text available from Highwire Press (Free Journals)
> http://highwire.stanford.edu/lists/freeart.dtl

This journal, not housed in the library, is found only by clicking on the hyperlink. We discuss this feature in Section, 2c.

Internet Sites

The catalog includes links to Internet sites that the librarians have identified as excellent academic resources, such as this government document:

> *Dietary Guidelines for Americans* [electronic resource]
> Washington, DC: Food and Nutrition Service, U.S. Dept. of Agriculture Internet access: Full text available from Health and Wellness Resource http://www.cnpp.usda.gov/Dietary Guideliness.htm

Reference Books

The electronic catalog also lists reference books. It indexes by call number those housed in the library. Those available online have hypertext links.

> *Essay and General Literature Index*
> H. W. Wilson Company
> Location: Reference Stacks, Level 2
> Call number: A13.E752
> Status: Available

> Social Sciences [electronic resource]
> Internet access: Full text available from Columbia International Affairs Online
> http://www.ciaonet.org/

Archives

Archival research takes you into past literature of a topic where you can trace developing issues and ideas on a subject.

Archives of Dermatology [electronic resource]
Internet access: Full text available from the American Medical
　　Association
http://archderm.ama-assn.org/

Bibliographies

Bibliographies list the works by a writer or the works about a subject.
They give you access to the titles of articles and books on your topic,
usually up to a certain date, as shown in the next example.

> *The Role of the Media in Promoting and Reducing Tobacco Use*
> National Cancer Institute, U.S. Dept of Health and Human
> Services
> Internet Access: http://www.tobacco.org/news/285317.html

HINT: Many college libraries as well as public libraries are
now part of a network of libraries. This network expands the
holdings of every library because one library will loan books
to another. Therefore, if a book you need is unavailable in
your library, ask a librarian about an interlibrary loan. Understand, however, that you may have to wait several days for its
delivery. Periodical articles usually come quickly by fax or
e-mail transfer.

2c Searching the Library's Electronic Databases

At the computer, search through the library's network of electronic
databases. You will find a list of these search engines at a link on the
library's home page, usually near the electronic book catalog. Each
one has a singular mission: to take you directly to articles on your
subject, with abstracts in most cases, and full text in many others.
Thus, you can print or download numerous documents, all relevant
to your subject. For example, InfoTrac is a popular database because
it covers many subjects. This list gives a few of the sources found
under the keyword *coffee*.

> *Does Coffee Cut Stroke Risk? NHS Choices* (Sept. 19, 2011) (1767
> words).
> *Full-Text*
>
> *Drink Up: Coffee May Combat Depression. Newsmax* (Sept. 27,
> 2011) (624 words)
> *Full-Text*

Coffee May Lower Risk of Fatal Prostate Cancer. Amanda Gardne.
AARP (May 18, 2011) (678 words).
Full-Text

Clicking on an underlined hypertext accesses the article for your use. Thus, you can print or download the information to your files. Remember to save them as text files.

General Databases

In addition to InfoTrac, there are many other general databases to serve your initial investigation. These databases are sometimes general in order to index many articles on a wide variety of topics. Start with one of these if you have a general keyword for your research but not a specific and focused topic.

BOOKS IN PRINT:	This database lists all books that are currently in print and available from publishers.
CQ RESEARCHER:	This collection provides in-depth reports on topics of current interest.
EBSCOHOST:	This database carries e-books on all subjects. To access a book online, you will need both a username and password, which are available from a librarian.
ENCYCLOPEDIA BRITANNICA:	This reference covers all subjects with brief, well-organized articles.
FIRSTSEARCH:	This database covers a wide variety of topics and directs you to both articles and books.
GPO:	This site for the Government Printing Office gives you access to all government publications on all subjects.
INFORME!:	This database offers an index to articles in Spanish-language magazines.
INGENTA CONNECT:	This site provides general information on a vast variety of topics. However, Ingenta Connect is a commercial site, and you will have to pay for articles that you download or order by fax.

ONLINE BOOKS PAGE:	Maintained by the University of Pennsylvania, this site gives you access to books on all subjects with options for printing or downloading the pages.
OXFORD REFERENCE ONLINE:	This database offers you the full text of 135 reference books from Oxford University Press. The sources cover all general subjects. See your librarian to secure the username and password necessary for entry into the database.

By investigating two or three of the databases listed above, you should gain a quick start on your initial investigation into a subject. The sources that you download or print will help you focus your topic and frame your thesis.

Databases by Discipline

Your library also houses subject-specific databases. Thus, you can examine a specialized database for articles on health issues or, if you prefer, history, and many others. Listed next, by subject area, are a few databases to help launch your investigation. *Note:* These sources are only available through library access, and in some cases they require an additional username and password that you must request from your librarian.

Literature

CONTEMPORARY LITERARY CRITICISM:	This database indexes critical articles about contemporary authors, thus it is a good source if you are examining the work of a twenty-first-century writer.
LITERATURE ONLINE (LION):	This database contains full-text poems, drama, and fiction. It also includes biographies, literary criticism, guides to analysis of literary works, and video readings by writers.
LITFINDER:	This source helps you find poems, stories, plays, and essays.
MLA INTERNATIONAL BIBLIOGRAPHY:	This major database provides access to all significant articles of criticism

on literature, linguistics, and
folklore.

History

AMERICA: HISTORY
AND LIFE: This is a first-rate database of
                            important articles on history.
HYPER HISTORY: This is a database of full-text articles
                            on all phases of world history.
VIVA: This database focuses on history with
                            an emphasis on women's studies.

Education, Psychology, and Social Issues

ERIC: This giant database takes you
                            quickly to articles and some books
                            with a focus primarily on education
                            but with full coverage of social and
                            communication topics.
PROJECT MUSE: This database contains current
                            issues of about 200 journals in the
                            fields of education, cultural studies,
                            political science, gender studies, lit-
                            erature, and others. It also links you
                            to JSTOR (see the next entry) for
                            past issues of the journals.
JSTOR: This acronym stands for "journal
                            storage" because this database
                            maintains the images of thousands
                            of academic articles in their origi-
                            nal form and with original page
                            numbers. It centers on the social
                            sciences but includes articles from
                            other fields, such as literature.
PSYCINFO: This database is a massive index
                            to articles and books in psychol-
                            ogy, medicine, education, and social
                            work.

Health, Medicine, Fitness, and Nutrition

CINAHL: The initials stand for *Cumulative
                            Index to Nursing & Allied Health
                            Literature.* The giant database

provides access to information in nursing, public health, and the allied fields of nutrition and fitness.

HEALTH AND WELLNESS: This database indexes a wide array of articles in medicine, nutrition, fitness, and public health.

PUBMED: This source indexes articles on dentistry as well as nursing and medicine.

The Arts

GROVE DICTIONARY OF ART: This source is an online art encyclopedia, not a database. It contains information from the *Dictionary of Art* and features about 45,000 articles on painting, sculpture, architecture, and other visual arts.

GROVE DICTIONARY OF MUSIC: Like the previous entry, this source is an online encyclopedia. It has 29,000 articles drawn from the printed versions of *New Grove Dictionary of Music and Musicians, New Grove Dictionary of Opera,* and *New Grove Dictionary of Jazz.* It covers the various aspects of music, such as instrumentation, orchestral performance, voice, and so forth.

MUSIC INDEX: This database provides a citation index to 655 journals on a broad range of musical topics, including reviews. However, it is a citation-only database, so no abstracts or full-text are provided. On that note, however, see the Hint on page 25.

Computers, Business, Technology

GENERAL BUSINESS FILE: This database provides abstracts and some full-text articles relating to issues in business and industry. It includes company profiles and some Wall Street reports.

SAFARI BOOKS ONLINE: This database focuses on e-commerce and computer science,

FAITS:	with information on programming and technology management. Faulkner Advisory of IT Studies is a database of articles on wireless communications, data networking, security, the Internet, and product comparisons.

The Physical Sciences

AGRICOLA:	This database provides an index to articles and book references in the areas of agriculture, animal, and plant sciences.
BIOONE:	This site provides articles on the biological, ecological, and environmental sciences.
GEOREF:	This database provides access to articles on geology and related subjects.
WILEY INTERSCIENCE:	This database has articles on science and biochemistry.

The databases described here represent just a portion of those available at most college libraries, and more databases are being added monthly. Your task is to determine which databases are available at your library and react accordingly. Obviously, small libraries will not have the online resources that you will find at the library of a major university. If databases are limited, you may need to consult the printed bibliographies and indexes, as discussed in Section 2d.

> **HINT:** If the databases to periodicals described in this section provide a citation but not the full text, you can probably retrieve the article in one of two ways: (1) try using the library's electronic book catalog (see 2b above) to retrieve the journal itself and thereby access the article, or (2) go into the stacks at your library, find the journal, and photocopy the article.

2d Searching the Printed Bibliographies

A bibliography tells you what books and articles are available for a specific subject. If you have a clearly defined topic, skip to page 26, "Searching in the Specialized Bibliographies and Reference Works."

If you are still trying to formulate a clear focus, begin with one of these general guides to titles of books to refine your search.

Searching in General Bibliographies

Some works are broad-based references to books on many subjects:

> *Bibliographic Index: A Cumulative Bibliography of Bibliographies* (in print and online).
> *Where to Find What: A Handbook to Reference Service Guide to Reference Books*

Figure 2.1 shows how *Bibliographic Index* sends you to bibliographic lists inside books. In this case, the bibliography is found on pages 278–279 of Wildavsky, Kelly, and Carey's book.

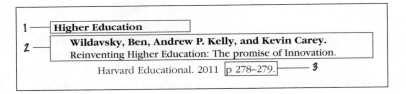

FIGURE 2.1
Example from *Bibliographic Index*, 2012, shows (1) subject heading, (2) entry of a book that contains a bibliography on higher education, (3) specific pages on which the bibliography is located.

If it fits your research, you would probably want to write a Works Cited entry for this source , as explained on pages 136–148. The MLA citation would look like this:

> Wildavsky, Ben, Andrew P. Kelly, and Kevin Carey. *Reinventing Higher Education: The Promise of Innovation*. Cambridge, MA: Harvard Educational, 2011. 278–79. Print.

Searching in the Specialized Bibliographies and Reference Works

After you have narrowed your subject, search one or two of the discipline-specific guides and bibliographies listed below. In the main, these are well-indexed references that will take you to more specific books. One of them can help you launch your investigation. Librarians at the reference desk can help you find them, and many are available online.

Humanities

Art	*Bibliographic Guide to Art and Architecture*
	Fine Arts: A Bibliographic Guide
Drama	*American Drama Criticism: Interpretations*
	Cambridge Guide to Theatre
History	*Dictionary of American History*
	America: History and Life
Literature	*Dictionary of Literary Biography*
	Essay and General Literature Index
Music	*Music Reference and Research Materials*
	Bibliographic Guide to Music
Philosophy	*Oxford Companion to Philosophy*
	Research Guide to Philosophy
Religion	*Reference Works for Theological Research*
	Who's Who in Religion

Social Sciences

Business	*Business and Economics Bibliographies*
	Encyclopedia of Business Information Sources
Education	*Education: A Guide to Reference and Information Sources*
	Resources in Education
Political Science	*Bibliography of Political Science*
	Theories of Political Process
Psychology	*Annual Review of Psychology*
	Psychology: A Guide to Reference and Information Sources
	Bibliographical Guide to Psychology
Sociology	*Social Workers' Desk Reference*
	Sociology: A Guide to Reference and Information Sources
Speech	*Research and Source Guide for Students in Speech Pathology and Audiology*
Women's Studies	*American Women Writers: A Critical Reference Guide*
	Women's Studies Index

Sciences

Astronomy	*The Cambridge Atlas of Astronomy*
	Dictionary of Astronomy
Biology	*Henderson's Dictionary of Biological Terms*
	Information Sources in the Life Sciences

Chemistry	*How to Find Chemical Information: A Guide for Practicing Chemists, Teachers, and Students*
	Lange's Handbook of Chemistry
Computer Science	*History of Computing Bibliography*
	Computer Science and Computing: A Guide to the Literature
Health	*Black's Medical Dictionary*
	Taber's Cyclopedic Medical Dictionary
Physics	*Information Sources in Physics*
	Physics Abstracts

2e   Searching the Printed Indexes

An index furnishes the exact page number(s) to articles in magazines, journals, and newspapers. When you have a well-developed idea of your topic, go to the specialized indexes of your discipline, such as *Music Index* or *Philosopher's Index* (either online at your library's computer or in print at the reference section of your library). If labeled an *index,* it may or may not include an abstract. If labeled as an index to *abstracts,* each entry will be an abstract. *Note:* An abstract is a brief description of an article, usually written by the author. An index to abstracts can accelerate your work by allowing you to read the abstract before you assume the task of locating and reading the entire work.

Starting with a General Index to Periodicals

A number of indexes are broad based and list articles in journals from many disciplines. These are good places to begin your research because the indexes have multiple entries and, in some cases, the articles are not as technical and scholarly as those indexed in specialized indexes. For general information on current events, consult *Readers' Guide to Periodical Literature,* which indexes such magazines as *Healthy Aging, Foreign Affairs, Psychology Today, American Scholar, Scientific Review,* and many others. An entry from *Readers' Guide to Periodical Literature* follows in Figure 2.2:

ANTIDEPRESSANTS
Mania in late life.
Felicity Richards and Martin Curtice. Advances in Psychiatric Treatment
v.17 p357–364 Sep 2011

■ FIGURE 2.2

From *Readers' Guide to Periodical Literature* showing subject, title, author, and publication data.

Make a bibliography entry for your research journal if it looks promising:

Richards, Felicity, and Martin Curtice. "Mania in Late Life."
    Advances in Psychiatric Treatment 17 (2011): 357–64. Print.

Searching Indexes to Topics in the Humanities

Arts and Humanities Citation Index (in print or online) catalogs more than 1,200 publications in several fields:

archaeology	folklore	performing arts
classical studies	history	philosophy
language and literature	literary criticism	religion
area studies	political criticism	theology

MLA International Bibliography (in print or online) indexes most of the journals in language and literature studies. The printed versions are not kept up to date, so supplement the printed version with the electronic database, if available.

Abstracts of English Studies (in print or online) provides an excellent place to begin research in literature studies.

Dissertation Abstracts International—A: Humanities and Social Sciences (in print or online) provides an index to the abstracts of all American dissertations. In the print version, look for issue No. 12, Part 11, of each volume, for it contains the cumulated subject and author indexes for Issues 1–12 of the volume's two sections.

Searching Indexes to Topics in the Social Sciences

Social Sciences Citation Index (in print or online) indexes journal articles for 263 periodicals in these fields:

anthropology	geography	political science
economics	law and criminology	psychology
environmental science	medical science	sociology

Dissertation Abstracts International—A: Humanities and Social Sciences (see above).

Searching Indexes to Topics in the Physical Sciences

Applied Science and Technology Index (in print or online) indexes articles in chemistry, engineering, computer science, electronics, geology, mathematics, photography, physics, and other related fields.

Biological and Agricultural Index (in print or online) indexes articles in biology, zoology, botany, agriculture, and related fields.

Dissertation Abstracts International—B: Sciences and Engineering (in print or online) provides an index to the abstracts of all American dissertations in the various fields of science and engineering. In the print version, look for issue No. 12, Part 11, of each volume, for it contains the cumulated subject and author indexes for Issues 1–12 of the volume's two sections.

Searching Indexes to Discipline-Specific Information

In addition to general indexes, you should examine indexes for your specific discipline. Numerous subject indexes are listed below in alphabetical order. Some will be available online through library access; others will be found in printed versions in the library's reference room.

Art Index
Biological Abstracts
*Business Periodicals
   Index*
Chemical Abstracts
*Communication
   Abstracts*
*Computer Literature
   Index*
Index of Economic Articles
Engineering Index
Environment Abstracts
Geo Abstracts
Historical Abstracts

Mathematical Reviews
Music Index
*Nursing and Allied Health
   Literature, Cumulative
   Index*
Philosopher's Index
Physical Education Index
Physics Abstracts
*Political Science
   Abstracts, International*
Psychological Abstracts
Religion Index One
Sociological Abstracts
Women's Studies Index

2f   Searching Biographies

Biographies of important people appear in books and articles, so you need to use a variety of sources. The electronic resources catalog (see 2b) is a place to start, using keywords such as "biography + index." It will access links to *Biography Index, Index to Literary Biography,* and many more. Alternatively, use the person's name as a keyword; for example, entering "Ben Franklin" will produce a reference to Cecil B. Currey's biography entitled *Ben Franklin: Patriot or Spy.*

In the library, examine these printed reference books:

Biography Index is a starting point for studies of famous persons. It will lead you to biographical information for people of all lands.

Current Biography Yearbook provides biographical sketches of important people. Most articles are three to four pages in length and include references to other sources at the end. It is current, thorough, and has international scope.

Contemporary Authors provides a biographical guide to current writers in fiction, nonfiction, poetry, journalism, drama, motion pictures, television, and a few other fields. It describes most contemporary writers. Entries include biographical facts, details on writings, and an overview of the author's work. A bibliography of additional sources is included.

Dictionary of Literary Biography provides a profile of thousands of writers in more than 100 volumes under such titles as *American Humorists, Victorian Novelists,* and *American Newspaper Journalists Biography.* A comprehensive index helps you locate the article on an author.

HINT: To find biographical reference works within a specific discipline, such as music or history, consult the library's electronic book catalog with a request such as "biographies of artists." It will then provide hyperlinks to *Who's Who in American Art* and other similar works.

2g   Searching Newspaper Indexes

Newspapers provide contemporary information. In the electronic catalog, search for a particular newspaper and then use its archival search engine to find articles on your topic. For example, asking for the Nashville *Tennessean* provides the link to the newspaper; by entering a search phrase, such as "state lottery," you gain access to articles in the current and previous editions of the *Tennessean,* as shown by the opening to the article in Figure 2.3:

Lawmaker: Home-schoolers shouldn't have tougher ACT mark
By DUREN CHEEK
Staff Writer

The **state**'s top lawyer was asked yesterday whether Tennessee's **lottery**-funded scholarship program is unconstitutional because it requires home-schooled students to meet higher standards than others entering college.

The request for an opinion came from **state** Rep. Glen Casada, R-College Grove, who said he thinks requiring home-schooled

---

FIGURE 2.3
Opening paragraphs of an article in *The [Nashville] Tennessean.*

students to score a 23 on their ACT to qualify, while public school students must score only 19, is unfair and discriminatory.

"Proponents of a **lottery** did not mention discriminating against home-schooled students in the **lottery** debate last fall,'" said Casada, referring to the **lottery** referendum last November. "Parents across the **state** were led to believe that students who met a certain criteria would receive a scholarship, period."

■■■ **FIGURE 2.3** (*Continued*)

If your library's electronic catalog cannot access your specific newspaper, go to the Internet at **www.newspapers.com**. See pages 47–48 for more information.

In your library, visit also the contemporary reading room where you will find current issues of local and national newspapers on display for your reading pleasure or for research.

2h   Searching the Indexes to Pamphlet Files

Librarians routinely clip items of interest from newspapers, bulletins, pamphlets, and miscellaneous materials and file them alphabetically by subject in loose-leaf folders. Make the pamphlet file a regular stop during preliminary investigation. Sometimes called the *vertical file,* it will have clippings on many topics, such as carpel tunnel syndrome, asbestos in the home, and medical care plans. Two helpful pamphlets, online and in print, are *SIRS* and *CQ Researcher.*

> *Social Issues Resources Series* (*SIRS*) collects articles on special topics and reprints them as one unit on a special subject, such as abortion, AIDS, prayer in schools, or pollution. With *SIRS* you will have ten or twelve articles readily available in one booklet.
>
> *CQ Researcher,* like *SIRS,* devotes one pamphlet to one topic, such as "Energy and the Environment." It will examine central issues on the topic, give background information, show a chronology of important events or processes, express an outlook, and provide an annotated bibliography.

■■■ **HINT:** For the correct citation forms to articles found in *SIRS* or *CQ Researcher*, see page 147.

2i Searching Government Documents

All branches of the government publish and make available valuable material. The GPO database, maintained by the Government Printing Office in Washington, DC, references this material. Your library may have this database, or you can access it on the Internet by entering **www.GPOAccess.gov** in your web browser (see "Government," page 00, for additional information). Just enter keywords in the search field to retrieve links to available documents. Your library might also house printed copies of these valuable reference tools:

> *Catalog of United States Government Publications* indexes all the documents published by the Government Printing Office.
>
> *Public Affairs Information Service Bulletin (PAIS)* indexes articles and documents published by miscellaneous organizations. Its excellent index makes it a good starting point.
>
> *Congressional Record* provides Senate and House bills, documents, and committee reports.
>
> *Public Papers of the Presidents of the United States* is the publication of the Executive Branch, including not only the president's papers but also the documents of all members of the president's cabinet and various agencies.
>
> *U.S. Code* is the publication of U.S. Supreme Court decisions, codes, and other rulings.

HINT: See pages 143–144 for instructions on how to write a Works Cited entry for government documents.

2j Searching for Essays within Books

The *Essay and General Literature Index* (online and in print) helps you find essays hidden within anthologies. It indexes material of both a biographical and a critical nature. The essay listed in the example below might easily have been overlooked by any researcher.

```
King, Martin Luther, 1929–1968
     Raboteau, A. J. Martin Luther King and the tradition of
black religious protest. (In Religion and the life of the nation;
ed. by R. A. Sherrill, p. 46–65).
```

The library's electronic book catalog will give you the call number to Sherrill's book.

2k Building Your Research Journal

By now, you should have a collection of printed documents, photocopies, and downloaded files. It is important that you keep everything in order with sources clearly marked because you will need to make citations in your text to the authors and page numbers, and you will need a Works Cited page that lists full information on each source. These may seem like obvious tasks to you, but reminders are helpful, and too many students have had to abandon perfectly good quotations because they could not find full data on the source for the Works Cited entry.

Build a computer folder. Create a folder on your hard drive to store all the information you download during your research. Use a flash drive when you conduct research at the labs and library. Each time you download an article, save it so you can copy it to your folder. As you gather more and more data and begin building an outline, you might create more than one research folder.

Name each file precisely. Be descriptive in naming your files so you can identify the content after a few days. A file named *Brown* offers no clue to its contents except that "Brown" is probably the name of the author of an article. Instead, describe the contents—for example, *BrownPesticidesandPets.*

Organize a print folder. You will need a notebook with sleeves to keep your written notes, printouts, and photocopies. This, too, should be organized along the lines of your outline.

Build a rough outline. Early on, write a rough outline to help you organize the mass of material you are gathering. It will also help identify topics needing more research. See pages 87–89 for additional details.

Build a Works Cited file. As you discover sources that fit your outline or sources that you have slotted into your rough draft, enter them in your Works Cited file in alphabetical order. Thus, you will accomplish a major task as you work your way through the project. This working bibliography should, at a minimum, contain the author's name, the title of the work, publication information, and a library call number if it is a book you have not yet examined. Shown below is an example, in MLA style, of one student's Works Cited file in progress with three entries.

Works Cited

LaFranchi, Howard. "Answering the World's Growing Water Problem." *Christian Science Monitor* 16 Apr. 2011. Web. 12 Oct. 2011.

Prud'homme, Alex. *The Ripple Effect: The Fate of Fresh Water in the Twenty-first Century.* New York: Scribner, 2011. Print.

"Water for Peace?" *Earth Island Journal* 26.1 (Spring 2011): 7. Print.

HINT: For other forms of bibliography entries, see the appropriate chapter for APA, CMS, and CSE styles in Chapters 11–13.

Gathering Sources Online

Clear Targets

Electronic sources are now a major basis of research information. The Internet makes available millions of computer files relating to any subject—articles, illustrations, sound and video clips, and raw data. This chapter provides direction for online searches:

- Searching for viable academic information on the web
- Accessing online sources
- Evaluating and filtering the complex web of Internet sites

Although the Internet cannot replace the references found in the library or field research, it offers the best and worst information, and requires careful evaluation. When reading an Internet article, always take time to judge its authority and veracity.

3a Beginning an Online Search

When you know your topic, perform a key search using the words you would like to find in the title, description, or text of an Internet source. For example, to find information on twenty-sixth President Theodore Roosevelt's foreign policies, you would enter the words *Theodore Roosevelt* and *foreign policy*. The search engine will direct you to a list of websites. You can then read the articles to determine if they relate to your research.

Using General Search Engines

About one hundred excellent search engines are available. Some of the more popular are listed below. Many sites entice you with advertisements for various products, but they do an excellent job of directing you to a wide variety of sources. Experiment with them and select the one that works best for you.

Subject directory search engines are compiled by humans and indexed to guide you to general areas that are then subdivided into specific categories. Your choice of a category controls the list.

About.com	http://www.about.com
Lycos	http://www.lycos.com
Yahoo!	http://www.yahoo.com

Robot-driven search engines perform a keyword search by electronically scanning millions of web pages. Your keyword phrase and Boolean operators control the list.

AltaVista	http://www.altavista.com
Bing	http://www.bing.com
Google	http://www.google.com

Find one you prefer, but keep in mind that search engines are designed in different ways. AltaVista, for example, will give you a massive number of results from its more than 22 million web pages. Yahoo!, on the other hand, is an edited site with directories and subdirectories.

Metasearch engines simultaneously query about ten major search engines, such as those listed above, and provide you with a short, relevant set of results. You get fewer results than would appear at one of the major search engines. For example, "chocolate + children" produced more than fifty million hits on Yahoo!, but only the top 100 links on Mamma.com. A metasearch engine selects the first few listings from each of the search engines under this theory: each engine puts the most relevant results at the top of its list. This theory may or may not be true. Here are three metasearch engines:

Dogpile	http://www.dogpile.com
Mamma.com	http://www.mamma.com
Metacrawler.com	http://www.metacrawler.com

HINT: Most web browser programs include a bookmark or favorites tool to allow you to save addresses of sites for quick access when revisiting the sites. Simply click on Bookmarks, then click on Add Bookmark to automatically add the URL to the list of bookmarks. In Microsoft Internet Explorer, use the button bar marked Favorites to record an address. Bookmarks can easily be titled and organized so that you could have a Bookmark file devoted to a list of sites related to your research paper. *Note:* If you are working at a university computer laboratory, do not add bookmarks to the hard drive. Instead, save the bookmarks to your zip or flash drive by using Save As in the File menu.

3b   Conducting Keyword and Boolean Searches

A **keyword** search uses words and phrases in the search field of a database or website search. Keywords are the descriptors or identifying words in a source's main title or the words that the author has identified as significant to the issue. Keywords provide straightforward access to databases and online resources. You may also use guided keyword search options to combine search elements, group terms, or select indexes or fields to be searched.

Advanced and **custom searches** utilize onscreen prompts for looking in a database or search engine. A guided search can also narrow the range of dates of publication, such as "after 2009" or "between 2007 and 2011." You can also narrow your choices in the search by format, such as only looking for periodicals and journal articles. For example, a search for sources that have the words *food dye* in their title and sources that use *hyperactivity* as another keyword would narrow the focus of the search.

Boolean expressions let you focus your keyword search by stipulating which words and phrases *can* appear in the results, which words *must* appear, or which topics *must not* appear in the search results. Most online databases and web search sites include the use of Boolean search terms, specifically *AND, OR,* and *NOT,* as well as the plus (+) or minus (−) signs. Placed between keywords, Boolean expressions instruct the search engine to display only those websites in which your research terms appear in certain combinations, and to ignore others.

- **AND or the "plus" (+) symbol:** This operator narrows the search by retrieving only records that contain both terms; hence, it narrows the focus of your search because both keywords must be found. Most search engines, such as Google and Yahoo!, will insert "and" or (+) automatically.

  Example: **food dye** is searched as **food + dye.**

- **Not or the "minus" (−) symbol:** This identifier excludes texts containing a specified word or phrase. The term "not" or the minus symbol finds sources that includes one term but not the other. If you want to eliminate "cancer" from your search about hyperactivity caused by food dye, add the word "NOT" to the search bar.

> Example: **food AND dye AND hyperactivity NOT cancer**

- **OR:** The operator "OR" broadens the search boundaries to include records containing more than one keyword. If you want to expand your search to include sources about food dye, hyperactivity, and allergies caused by food dye, use the conjunction "OR" to add more focus to the source articles listed in your search.

> Example: **food AND dye AND hyperactivity OR allergy**

- **Quotation marks (" "):** Placing search terms inside quotation marks will signal the database or search engine to match your exact word order on the web document. Placing "food dye" inside quotation marks, for example, will result in sources that only contain the exact phrase.

> Example: **"food dye" AND "hyperactivity"**

- **Wildcard searches** use truncated symbols to explore the varied forms of a basic, root word. Rather than conducting several searches for the same basic word—such as *child, children, childhood,* and so on—you can focus your keyword search to find a term with variant spelling or endings by using an asterisk (*) or a question mark (?) as the wildcard or truncation symbol.

The asterisk (*) usually takes the place of one or more characters at the end of a word.

> Example: **diet***   Results: **diet, diets, dietary, dietician, dietetics**

The question mark (?) usually takes the place of a single character in a word.

> Example: **ne?t**   Results: **neat, nest, next**

Some systems use wildcard symbols such as **(!), ($), or (:)**. Consult the help section in a library database or Internet search site to learn which wildcard symbols are supported.

3c Using Search Engines Devoted to Academic Disciplines

Many search engines specialize in one area, such as Edweb (education studies) or Envirolink (environmental studies). The following list contains sites that may be helpful in launching your investigation of Internet resources.

Humanities

Art

Art Resource **http://www.artres.com/c/htm/Home.aspx** This site features the world's largest stock photo archive with a keyword-searchable index.

World Wide Arts Resources **http://www.wwar.com** This site provides an artist index as well as an index to exhibits, festivals, meetings, and performances. Its search engine will take you to fine arts departments, online courses, syllabi, and art institutions.

History

Archiving Early America **http://www.earlyamerica.com** This site provides images of eighteenth-century documents for reading and downloading, such as the Bill of Rights and the speeches of Washington, Paine, Jefferson, and others.

The History Net **http://www.historynet.com/** This site provides resources in the humanities and social sciences with links to wars and conflicts, air and sea battles, cultural studies, discovery, and exploration.

Literature

EServer **http://eserver.org/** This site provides academic resources in the humanities, including drama, fiction, film, television, and history.

Open Directory Project **http://www.dmoz.org/Arts/Literature/** This site provides a directory, with links, to specific pieces of literature.

Voice of the Shuttle **http://vos.ucsb.edu/** This site provides access to a massive collection of literary bibliographies, textual criticism, newsgroups, and links to classical studies, history, philosophy, and other related disciplines.

Philosophy

The American Philosophical Association Internet site **http://www.apaonline.org.** This site provides articles, bibliographies, software, a bulletin board, gopher server, and links to other philosophical sites containing college courses, journals, texts, and newsletters.

Episteme Links: Philosophy Resources on the Internet **http://www.epistemelinks.com/.** This site offers links to issues, traditions, biographies, philosophical movements, and full-text works.

> **HINT:** If you have problems accessing a particular site, try truncating the address by cutting items from the end. For example, cut **http://www.emory.edu/WHSC/medweb.medlibs.html** to **http://www.emory.ed.** At this main page of the website, you can go in search of whatever site-related information you need.

Religion

Interfaith Online **http://www.interfaith.org** This comprehensive site gives references and resources on all religions and religious studies and religious organizations.

Vanderbilt Divinity School **http://divinity.library.vanderbilt.edu/** A valuable source of references to and interpretations of the Bible, this site links to other religious websites and online journals, such as *Biblical Archaeologist.*

Social Sciences

Business

Academy of International Business (AIB) **http://aib.msu.edu/.** This is the leading association of scholars and specialists in the field of international business. Representing more than eighty different countries, members include scholars from many academic institutions as well as consultants and researchers.

Global Edge **http://globaledge.msu.edu/ibrd/ibrd.asp** This link takes you to hundreds of articles and resource materials on banks, insurers, market news, jobs, and miscellaneous data for students.

Communication

Communication Resources on the World Wide Web **http://www.lib.utsa.edu/Research/Subject/communicationguide.html** This large database takes you to resources and websites on associations, book reviews, bibliographies, libraries, media, information science programs, and departments of communication in various universities.

Education

Educause **http://www.educause.com/** This site focuses on educational and information technology. It has full-text articles from *Educause Review* and *Educause Quarterly.*

Edweb **http://www.edwebproject.org/resource.cntnts.html**
This site focuses on educational issues and resource materials
for grades K–12, with articles on web education, web history,
and web resources.

ERIC (Educational Resource and Information Center) **http://
www.eric.ed.gov/** ERIC is considered the primary source of
research information for most educators. It contains about
one million documents, available by a keyword search, on all
aspects of teaching and learning, administration, and almost
any topic related to the classroom. It includes lesson plans
and bibliographies.

Government

Fedworld **http://www.fedworld.gov/** This site links to websites
of federal government departments as well as lists of helpful
articles. It links to the Internal Revenue Service and other
government agencies.

Library of Congress **http://www.loc.gov/index.html** This site
provides access to the Library of Congress catalog online for
books by author, subject, and title. It also links to historical
collections and research tools, such as "Thomas," which provides access to congressional legislation.

White House Web **http://www.whitehouse.gov** This site provides a graphical tour, messages from the president and
the vice president, and accounts of life at the White House.
Visitors to this site can even leave a message for the president
in the guest book.

Political Science

Political Science Resources **https://liberty.wpunj.edu/library/
Resources/PoliticalScience.html** Sponsored by William
Patterson University, this site provides a vast number of links
to general sources for political science resources as well as
American government and politics.

Psychology

Encyclopedia of Psychology **http://www.psychology.org/
links/Resources/Doing_Research/** This site features a collection of articles for preparing psychology documents from
research. It has current and archival information.

PsycINFO **http://www.apa.org/databases/psychinfo/index
.aspx** The American Psychological Association maintains this

excellent site of current and archival information in the various behavioral disciplines.

Sociology

Intute: Social Sciences **http://www.intute.ac.uk/socialsciences/ lost.html** This site provides keyword access to websites in the social sciences.

Sociology **http://hakatai.mcli.dist.maricopa.edu/smc/ml/ sociology.html** This site gives access to numerous sites that provide articles and resource materials on almost all aspects of sociology issues.

Women's Studies

Women's Resource Project **http://www.ibiblio.org/cheryb/ women/** This site links to libraries on the web that have collections on women's studies. It also has links to women's programs and women's resources on the web.

Women's Studies Database **http://www.mith2.umd.edu/ WomensStudies/** This site features a search engine for keyword searching women's issues and links to bibliographies, classic texts, references, course syllabi from various universities, and gateways to several other websites.

Sciences

Astronomy

American Astronomical Society **http://aas.org** This site has the full text of the *Astrophysical Journal,* providing articles, reviews, and educational information. The site also provides links to other astronomical sites on the web.

Science at NASA **http://science.nasa.gov/Astronomy.htm** This site links to NASA programs, such as the International Space Station or Project Galileo. It provides maps of the planets, views of Earth from many different angles, and plenty of planetary information.

Computer and Internet Technology

Computer Science: A Guide to Web Resources **http://libguides .library.albany.edu/csci** This site is a good starting point for students because it provides numerous links to resources in the discipline.

Internet Society http://www.isoc.org/ This site is supported by the companies, agencies, and foundations that launched the Internet and that keep it functioning. It gives vital information published in the ISOC Forum newsletter.

Information Technology Services http://www.utexas.edu/its/services/network/ This site gives access to Internet and networking centers and relevant books, articles, and bibliographies.

Environmental Science

Envirolink http://envirolink.org This site has a search engine that provides access to environmental articles, photographs, action alerts, organizations, and additional web sources.

The Virtual Library of Natural Sciences and Mathematics http://vlib.org/Science This site provides valuable links to other websites in categories such as endangered species, global sustainability, and pollution.

General Science

The Academy of Natural Sciences http://www.ansp.org/library/index.php This site has links to hundreds of articles and resource materials on various issues and topics in the natural sciences.

Thomson Reuters Scientific http://science.thomsonreuters.com This site provides searchable databases in biology and life sciences and serves as an excellent resource for students wishing to conduct scientific research.

The National Academies http://www.nas.edu This comprehensive site combines the resources of the National Academy of Sciences and Engineering, the Institute of Medicine, and the National Research Council. It focuses on math and science education, and it has links to scientific societies.

Health and Medicine

Global Health http://www.globalhealth.gov/ This site provides articles on environmental destruction, overpopulation, infectious diseases, the consequences of war, and, in general, the health of the globe. It offers links to other journals, newsletters, and government documents that explore environmental issues.

Health Sciences Library **http://health.library.emory.edu/** The Health Sciences Library at Emory University provides a site that connects you with medical libraries and their storehouses of information. It also gives links to other health-related communities and connections.

National Institutes of Health **http://www.nih.gov** NIH leads the nation in medical research, so this site provides substantive information on numerous topics, from cancer and diabetes to malpractice and medical ethics. It provides links to online journals for the most recent news in medical science.

HINT: You can quickly build a bibliography using the Internet in two ways: (1) at a search engine such as Google, enter a descriptive phrase, such as "child abuse bibliographies," and (2) at **http://www.amazon.com** and **http://www.barnesandnoble.com**, gather a list of books currently in print. Then, go in search of the books at your library.

3d Accessing Online Sources

Several types of online sources are available, and you should use more than one type in your research.

Internet Home Pages

You can locate home pages for individuals, institutions, and organizations by using a search engine, such as Yahoo! or Google (see page 37), as explained in Section 3a, "Beginning an Online Search." Just type in a person's name or the name of an organization in the search field. For example, a search for the American poet James Dickey will get a link to the site **http://www.jamesdickey.org/**. A home page will provide links, a directory, an index, and an internal search engine that will take you quickly to specific material.

Internet Articles on the Web

A search engine will direct you to many articles on the web, some isolated without documentation and credentials and others that list the author as well as the association to which the author belongs. For example, a search for "child care centers" will produce local sites, such as "Apple Tree Family Child Care." Private sites like these will infuse local knowledge to your research. Adding another relevant term, such as "child care regulations," will take you to state and national sites, such as the National Resource Center for Health and Safety in Child Care.

> **HINT:** An Internet article that contains only a title and the URL cannot be properly documented and should be avoided.

Journal Articles on the Web

The Internet supplies journal articles of two types: (1) articles in online journals designed and published only on the web, and (2) reproductions of articles that have appeared in printed journals. Find them in three ways.

- Using your favorite search engine, enter a keyword phrase for *journals* plus the name of your subject. For example, one student using Google entered a keyword search for "journals + fitness" and found links to twenty journals devoted to fitness, such as *Health Page, Excite Health,* and *Physical Education.*
- Access a search engine's subject directory. In Yahoo!, for example, one student selected "Social Science" from the key directory, clicked on Sociology, clicked on Journals, and accessed links to several online journals, such as *Sociological Research Online* and *Edge: The E-Journal of Intercultural Relations.*
- If you already know the name of a journal, go to your favorite search engine to make a keyword query, such as *PsychNology.*

Note: Some journals will furnish an abstract but then require a fee for access to the full text. The journals may also be available in library databases.

> **HINT:** Remember that abstracts may not accurately represent the full article. In fact, some abstracts are not written by the author at all but by editorial staff. Resist the desire to copy quotations from the abstract; instead, write a paraphrase or, better, find the full text and cite from it.

Magazine Articles on the Web

The Internet supplies magazine articles of two types. Some appear in original online magazines designed and published only on the web. Others are reproductions of articles that have appeared in printed magazines. Several directories exist for finding magazine articles:

> MagazineDirectory.com **http://www.magazine-directory .com/** This site has directories of magazine home page links. Under "current events," for example, are *Atlantic Monthly* at theatlantic.com, *Harper's* at Harpers.org, and *Time* at time. com/time/. A magazine's archives can be searched at its site.
>
> HighBeam Research **http://www.highbeam.com/** This website has a subscription-based search engine to 17 million documents in newspapers, magazines, and news services. Free access is available for seven days; charges will accrue if membership is not canceled.
>
> Pathfinder **http://pathfinder.com/** This site gives free access to *Time Magazine* and thousands of archival articles.
>
> ZD Net **http://www.zdnet.com/** This site provides access to industry-oriented articles in banking, electronics, computers, and management. It offers two weeks of free access before charges begin to accrue.

You can also access online magazines through a search engine's directory. For example, using AltaVista, you can click on "Health and Fitness" in the subject directory of the home page, click next on "publications," and then "magazines." The result is a list of forty magazines devoted to various aspects of health and fitness, such as *Healthology* and *The Black Health Net*.

News Sources

Most major news organizations maintain Internet sites. Consult one of these:

> CNN Interactive **http://www.cnn.com/** This site features a good search engine that takes you quickly without cost to transcripts of its broadcasts. It is a good source for research in current events.
>
> C-SPAN Online **http://www.c-span.org/** This site emphasizes public affairs and offers both a directory and a search engine to transcripts. It is a valuable source for research in public affairs, government, and political science.
>
> CQ Press Electronic Library **http://library.cqpress.com/ index.php/** This site keeps tabs on congressional activities in Washington.

National Public Radio Online **http://www.npr.org/** This site provides audio articles downloaded using RealPlayer, Windows Media Player, or some other audio engine. Be prepared to take careful notes.

The New York Times on the Web **http://www.nytimes.com/** This site provides free access to recent articles. However, there is a fee for articles found in the 365-day archive. After purchase, articles appear on the monitor for printing or downloading.

USA Today DeskTopNews **http://www.usatoday.com/** This site has a fast search engine and provides information about current events.

U.S. News Online **http://www.usnews.com/** This site has a fast search engine and provides free, in-depth articles on current political and social issues.

The Washington Times **http://www.washtimes.com/** This site has up-to-the-minute political news.

To find additional newspapers, search for "newspapers" on Yahoo! or Google. Your college library may also provide LEXIS-NEXIS, which will search online news sources for you.

HINT: Provide documentation to the Internet source to avoid the appearance of citing from the printed version. Major differences often exist between the same article in *USA Today* and in *USA Today* DeskTopNews.

Books on the Web

One of the best sources of full-text, online books is the Online Books Page at the University of Pennsylvania: **http://digital .library.upenn.edu/books/**. This site indexes books by author, title, and subject. Its search engine takes you quickly to the full text of Thomas Hardy's *A Pair of Blue Eyes* or Linnea Hendrickson's *Children's Literature: A Guide to the Criticism*. This site adds new textual material almost every day, so consult it first. Understand, however, that contemporary books, still under copyright protection, are not included. That is, you can freely download an Oscar Wilde novel, but not one by contemporary writer J. K. Rowling. Here are a few additional sites:

Bartleby.com   **http://www.bartleby.com/**
Internet Classics Archive **http://classics.mit.edu/**

Project Gutenberg	http://promo.net/pg/
Bibliomania	http://www.bibliomania.com/
Lesson Planet	http://www.lessonplanet.com/
American Literary Classics	http://www.americanliterature.com/

There are many more; in a search engine, use a keyword request for "full-text books."

Browsing Wikis, Blogs, Listserv, Usenet, and Chat Groups

Although they can supply current information, online sources such as electronic mailing lists, newsgroups, blogs, and wikis are collaborative projects that cannot guarantee the expertise of their information. Most of these sources do not have a group moderator; hence, they post everything from expert data and testimony to opinions given by persons who are not experts in your field of study. Always be wary and approach these sources with cynicism as you identify true and accurate information.

E-mail Discussion Groups

Discussion groups correspond by e-mail on a central topic. For example, your literature professor might ask everybody in the class to join an e-mail discussion group on Victorian literature. To participate, you must have an e-mail address and subscribe to the list. Special forums can be designated that request the response of all members in the class. Your participation will often contribute to your final grade.

Real-time chatting is also available through immediate messages on the Internet or with members of chat groups. However, we discourage the use of chat commentary for your research. Even though Yahoo!, MSN, Lycos, and other servers offer access to chat groups, you cannot quote people with fictional usernames and no credentials. If you are fortunate enough to enter a scholarly discussion on your topic, you might obtain useful information. Consult one of the following search engine directories for mailing lists, newsgroups, and discussion forums:

CyberFiber	http://www.cyberfiber.com/
Google Groups	http://groups.google.com/
Newzbot	http://www.newzbot.com/
Tile.Net	http://tile.net/lists

CHECKLIST

Evaluating Internet Sources

- Generally, using "edu" and "org" sites is preferable to using "com" sites because these domains usually are developed by an educational institution, such as Ohio State University, or by a professional organization, such as the American Psychological Association. Be sure to check authorship, currency, and other credentials. The "gov" (government) and "mil" (military) sites also usually have reliable materials.

- The "com" (commercial) sites become suspect for several reasons: (1) they are selling advertising space, (2) they often charge you for access to their files, and (3) they can be ISP (Internet service provider) sites where people pay to post material that has not been edited and subjected to peer review.

- What is the date? References in the sciences demand a date because research becomes out of date quickly. In like manner, look for the date when the web information was last revised.

- Look for the professional affiliation of the writer, which you will find in the opening credits, or an e-mail address. Ask this question: Is the writer affiliated with a professional organization? Information should be included in the opening credit. An e-mail address might also show academic affiliation. Is contact information for the author or sponsoring organization included in the document? Other ways to investigate the credibility of a writer are searching for the writer's home page and by looking on Amazon for a list of his or her books.

- Can you identify the target audience? What does that tell you about the purpose of the website? Remember, the websites needed for your research should appeal to the intellectual person.

- What bias colors the website? *Note:* There will be a bias of some sort because even academic sites show bias toward, for example, the grandeur of Greek philosophy, the brilliance of the Allied Forces in World War II, or the artistry of Picasso's Blue period.

- Look at the end of Internet articles for a bibliography of sources that indicate the scholarly nature of this writer's work.

- Treat e-mail as mail correspondence when using it as a scholarly source. Be sure the writer has solid credentials. Additionally, academic discussion groups may sometimes contain valuable information, but use it only if you know the source of the discourse.

- Do not cite from chat forums where fictitious usernames are common.

- Hypertext links to educational sites serve as an academic bibliography to reliable sources. However, if the site gives you hypertext links to commercial sites or if pop-up advertisements flood the screen, abandon the site and do not quote from it.

- Learn to distinguish among the different types of websites, such as advocacy pages, personal home pages, informational pages, and business and marketing pages. One site provides several evaluation techniques that might prove helpful: **http://www.lib.berkeley.edu/ TeachingLib/Guides/Internet/Evaluate.html**.

- Your skills in critical reading and thinking can usually determine the validity of a site. For more information on critical reading, visit this site: **http://www.virtualsalt .com/**.

4

Conducting Field Research

Clear Targets

Each discipline has different expectations in its methods of inquiry and presentation. This chapter provides a variety of field research techniques:

- Researching within a discipline
- Investigating local sources
- Conducting surveys and experiments

The human species is distinguished by its ability to examine the world systematically and to create pioneers for the new millennium, such as computer technicians, microsurgeons, and nuclear engineers. Through field research you may become one of them.

4a | Conducting Research within a Discipline

Some disciplines, more than others, will require you to work in the laboratory or the field, not just the library. Attitudes and methods differ in the social, physical, and applied sciences, and those three differ in many ways from the attitudes and methods of humanists.

The Social Scientists

Social scientists work from the assumption that behavior can be observed, tested, and cataloged by observation and experimental testing. Professionals perform thousands of experiments every month. They research stress in the workplace, study the effects of birth order on the youngest child, and develop testing mechanisms, such as the SAT test. As a student in the social sciences, you will be asked to perform similar but less exhaustive studies, such as observing "the typing mannerisms of students composing on a computer." If your topic examines any aspect of human behavior (for example, "road rage on campus streets"), prepare to go into the field for some aspects of your research.

The Physical Scientists

Physical scientists wish to discover, define, and explain the natural world. They operate under the assumption that we can obtain precise data on flora and fauna, geological formations, the various species of animals, and so forth. You may be asked to join a field expedition to catalog one type of fern, to test the water conditions at a local lake, or to locate sinkholes in a confined area. Laboratory experimentation is also a regular feature for scientists. Any experiments that you conduct should be recorded in a lab notebook because they may become significant to your written reports. If your topic examines the natural world in some way—for example, "the growing deer population in Governor's Manor subdivision"—field research may be useful.

The Applied Scientists

Applied scientists *apply* the knowledge they acquire to make life more efficient, enduring, and comfortable. By mathematical formulas and cutting-edge technology, they launch spaceships to encircle the globe, find new ways to repair broken bones, and discover better methods of movie animation. You, too, can participate in such experiments by designing access facilities for students with wheelchairs (for example, should doors open out or open in?), investigating systems to measure the force of lightning strikes, or examining ways to increase the weight of beef cattle. It is not unusual today for undergraduate students to apply their computer knowledge to the creation of new programs, even new software and hardware. If your research involves application of scientific information, researching in the field may help you formulate your ideas.

The Humanists

Humanists in the fine arts, literature, history, religion, and philosophy have a distinctive approach to knowledge. While scientists usually investigate a small piece of data and its meaning, humanists examine an entire work of art (Verdi's opera *Rigoletto*), a period of history (the Great Depression), or a philosophical theory (existentialism). Humanists usually accept a poem or painting as a valid entity and search it subjectively for what it means to human experience. However, that fact does not preclude humanists from conducting field research. For example, a student might go to England to retrace the route of the pilgrims in their journey to Canterbury. Such a trip might shed new light on Chaucer's poetry. In another instance, a student's field trip to Jackson, Mississippi, might enlighten the scholar on the fiction of Eudora Welty. Conducting archival research on manuscript materials could take you into unknown territory. Your work with a writer living in your locality may prompt you toward a personal interview. And correspondence with writers and historians is standard fare in humanist research. Thus, if your research in history, religion, or the arts offers the opportunity for field research, add it to your research program.

4b   Investigating Local Sources

Interviewing Knowledgeable People

Talk to persons who have experience with your subject. Personal interviews can elicit valuable in-depth information. They provide information that few others will have. Look to organizations for experienced persons. For example, a student writing on a folklore topic might contact the county historian, a senior citizens organization, or a local historical society. If necessary, the student could post a notice soliciting help: "I am writing a study of local folklore. Wanted: people who have knowledge of regional tales." Another way to accomplish this task is to request information from an e-mail discussion group, which will bring responses from several persons (see page 49 for more details).

Follow a few general guidelines:

- Set up your appointments in advance.
- Consult with persons knowledgeable about your topic.
- If possible, talk to several people to get a fair assessment.
- A telephone interview is acceptable, as is e-mail correspondence.
- Be courteous and arrive on time for interviews.
- Be prepared in advance with a set of focused, relevant questions.
- For accuracy, and if permitted by the person being interviewed, record the session with an audio or videotape.
- Double-check direct quotations with the interviewee or the tape.
- Get permission before citing a person by name or quoting the person's exact words.
- Handle private and public papers with great care, and send participants a copy of your report along with a thank-you note.

When finished, make a Works Cited entry just as you would for a book:

> Thornbright, Mattie Sue. "Growing Greens in Georgia." Personal
> interview. Jonesboro, Georgia. 15 Jan. 2012. MS.

Writing Letters and Corresponding by E-mail

Correspondence provides a written record for research. Write a letter that asks pointed questions that will elicit relevant responses. Tell the person who you are, what you are attempting to do, and why you have chosen to write to this specific person.

Make your message a fairly specific request for a minimum amount of information. It does not require an expansive reply. If you use a quotation from the reply, provide a bibliography entry on the Works Cited page.

> Casasola, Evelyn. Principal of Parkview Elementary School,
> Topeka, KS. Message to the author. 5 Apr. 2012. E-mail.

Reading Personal Papers

Search out letters, diaries, manuscripts, family histories, and other personal materials that might contribute to your study. The city library may house private collections, and the public librarian might help you contact the county historian and other private citizens who have important documents. Obviously, handling private papers must be done with the utmost decorum and care. Make a Works Cited entry for such materials.

> Joplin, Barry. "Notes on Robert Penn Warren." Unpublished
> paper. Nashville. 19 Oct. 2012. MS.

Attending Lectures and Public Addresses

Watch bulletin boards and the newspaper for a public speaker who may contribute to your research. At the lecture, take careful notes, and if the speaker makes one available, secure a copy of the lecture or speech. If you want to use your equipment to make an audio or videotape of a speech, courtesy demands that you seek permission. Remember that many lectures, reproduced on video, are available in the library or in departmental files. Always make a Works Cited entry for any words or ideas you use.

> Petty-Rathbone, Virginia. "Edgar Allan Poe and the Image of
> Ulalume." Lecture. Heard Library, Vanderbilt U., 25 Jan.
> 2012. Address.

Investigating Government Documents

Documents are available at four levels of government: city, county, state, and federal. As a constituent, you are entitled to examine a wide assortment of records on file at various agencies. If your topic demands it, you may contact the mayor's office, attend and take notes at a meeting of the county commissioners, or search for documents in the archives of the state or federal government.

City and County Government

Visit the courthouse or county clerk's office to find facts on elections, marriages, births, and deaths, as well as census data. Local archives include house wills, tax rolls, military assignments, deeds to property, and much more. A trip to the local courthouse can help you trace the history of the land and its people.

State Government

Contact a state office that relates to your research, such as Consumer Affairs (general information), the Public Service Commission (which regulates public utilities such as the telephone company), or the Department of Human Services (which administers social and welfare services). The name of these agencies may vary from state to state. Each state has an archival storehouse and makes its records available for public review.

Federal Government

The Government Printing Office provides booklets and publications. A list of these materials, many of which are free, appears on the website of the government printing office, www.GPOAccess.gov. In addition, you can visit the National Archives Building in Washington, DC, or one of the regional branches in Atlanta, Boston, Chicago, Denver, Fort Worth, Kansas City, Los Angeles, New York, Philadelphia, or Seattle. Their archives contain court records and government documents. Before going, review the *Guide to the National Archives of the United States, Select List of Publications of the National Archives and Record Service,* and the *Catalog of National Archives Microfilm Publications.*

4c   Examining Audiovisual Materials, the Internet, and Television

Important data can be found in audiovisual materials. You will find these both on and off campus. Consult guides such as *Educators Guide* (film, filmstrips, and tapes), *Media Review Digest* (nonprint materials), *Video Source Book* (video catalog), *The Film File,* or *International Index to Recorded Poetry* to find relevant titles. Television, with its many channels, such as *the History Channel,* offers invaluable data in programs that you can record for later detailed examination. The Internet, as discussed earlier, provides multimedia on almost every conceivable topic. As with other sources, write Works Cited entries for any materials that have merit and contribute to your paper.

> "Debate 101: It's Like a Job Interview." Narr. Gloria Borger.
> CNN. Cable News Network. 18 Oct. 2011. Television.

When using media sources, watch closely the opening and closing credits to capture the necessary data for your Works Cited entry. The format is explained on pages 147–148. As with the personal interview, be scrupulously accurate in taking notes. Citations may refer to a performer, director, or narrator, depending on the focus of your study. It is best to write direct quotations because paraphrases of television commentary can unintentionally be distorted by bias. Always scrutinize material taken from an Internet site (see pages 50–51 for a checklist of ways to evaluate Internet articles).

Conducting a Survey with a Questionnaire

Questionnaires can produce current, firsthand data that you can tabulate and analyze. To achieve meaningful results, you must survey randomly with regard to age, sex, race, education, income, residence, and other demographic factors. Bias can creep into the questionnaire unless you remain objective. Use a formal survey only if you are experienced with tests and measurements and statistical analysis or when you have an instructor who will help you with the instrument. Be advised that most schools have a Human Subjects Committee that sets guidelines, draws up consent forms, and requires anonymity of participants for information gathering that might be intrusive. An informal survey gathered in the hallways of campus buildings lacks credibility in the research paper. If you build a table or graph from the results, see page 209 in the appendix for an example.

Surveys usually depend on *quantitative* methodologies, which produce numerical data. That is, the questionnaire results can be tallied to itemize such things as campus crime rates, parking slots for students, or the shift in student population to off-campus housing. In some cases, surveys depend on *qualitative* methodologies, which answer questions on social issues, such as the number of biased words in a history text, the reasons for marijuana use, or levels of hyperactivity in a test group of children.

Reference your project survey in the Works Cited section of your paper.

> Castor, Diego, and Carmen Aramide. "Child Care Arrangements of
> Parents Who Attend College." Coeur d'Alene: North Idaho
> College, 2012. Survey.

Keep the questionnaire short, clear, and focused on your topic. Questions must be unbiased. Ask your professor to review the instrument before using it. Design your questionnaire for a quick response to a scale ("Choose A, B, or C"), to a ranking (first choice, second choice, and so on), or to fill-in blanks. You should also arrange for an easy return of the questionnaire by providing a self-addressed stamped envelope or by allowing respondents to submit the survey online.

Tabulate the responses objectively. Present the results—positive or negative—as well as a sample questionnaire in the appendix to your paper. While results that deny your hypothesis may not support the outcome you desire, they still have value.

4e　Conducting Experiments, Tests, and Observation

Empirical research, performed in a laboratory or in the field, can determine why and how things exist, function, or interact with one another. Your paper will explain your methods and findings in pursuit of a hypothesis or theory. An experiment thereby becomes primary evidence for your paper.

Observation occurs generally in the field, which might be at a child care center, a movie theater, a parking lot, or the counter of a McDonald's restaurant. The field is anywhere you can observe, count, and record behavior, patterns, and systems. It can be testing the water in a stream or observing the nesting patterns of deer. Retail merchandisers conduct studies to observe buying habits. A basketball coach might gather and analyze shot selections by members of his team.

A *case study* is a formal report based upon your observation of a human subject. For it, you might have to examine patterns of behavior to build a profile. It can be based on biographical data, interviews, tests, and observation. For example, you might observe and interview an older person with dementia, and that would be a case study and evidence for your research paper. Each discipline has its own standards for properly conducting a case study. You should not examine any subject without the guidance and approval of your instructor.

Most experiments and observations begin with a *hypothesis,* which is similar to a thesis (see pages 9–11 for more details). The hypothesis is a statement assumed to be true for the purpose of investigation. *Hummingbirds live as extended families governed by a patriarch* is a hypothesis needing data to prove its validity. *The majority of people will not correct the poor grammar of a speaker* is a hypothesis that needs testing and observation to prove its validity.

You can begin observation without a hypothesis and let the results lead you to the implications. Shown below is one student's double-entry format used to record observation on the left and commentary on the right. It is a limited example of field notes.

Record:	Response:
Day 1	
10-minute session at window, three hummingbirds fighting over the feeder	Is the male chasing away the female or is the female the aggressor?
Day 2	
10-minute session at window, saw eight single hummingbirds at feeder #1 and one guarding feeder #2 by chasing others away	I did some research and the red-throated male is the one that's aggressive.

Generally, a report on an experiment or observation follows a format that provides four distinct parts: introduction, method, results, and discussion. These four divisions of the scientific report are discussed fully in Section 7a, pages 83–84.

CHECKLIST

Conducting an Experiment or Observation

- Express clearly your hypothesis in the introduction.
- Provide a review of the literature if necessary for establishing an academic background for the work.

- Explain your design for the study-lab experiment, observation, or the collection of raw data in the field.
- Design the work for maximum respect to your subjects. In that regard, you may find it necessary to get approval for your research from a governing board.
- For the results section, maintain careful records and accurate data. Don't let your expectations influence the results.
- Be prepared in your conclusion to discuss your findings and any implications to be drawn.

5

Understanding and Avoiding Plagiarism

Clear Targets

Intellectual property has value; hence, there are ethical standards for writing in an academic environment. The purpose of this chapter is to define and explore the ethics of research writing:

- Using sources to enhance your credibility
- Using sources to place a citation in its proper context
- Honoring property rights and crediting sources

By studying examples of careful documentation as well as plagiarism, we can discover the worst and best of research projects and citing borrowed material. Moreover, we must face the constant problem of the Internet, which makes it easy to copy and download material and paste it into a paper.

5a Using Sources to Enhance Your Credibility

What some students fail to realize is that citing a source in their papers, even the short ones, signals something special and positive to readers—that the student has researched the topic, explored the literature about it, and has the expertise to share it. By announcing clearly the name of a source, the writer reveals the scope of his or her critical reading in the literature, as shown in these notes by one student:

> Americans consume an average of 300-plus liters of water per day per capita while the average person needs only 20 to 40 liters, according to O'Malley and Bowman.

> Sandra Postel says water is "a living system that drives the workings of a natural world we depend on" (19).

Postel declares: "A new water era has begun" (24). She indicates that the great prairies of the world will dry up, including America's. Hey, when folks in America notice the drought, then maybe something will happen.

If transferred into the paper, these notes will enable readers to identify the sources used. The notes give clear evidence of the writer's investigation into the subject, and they enhance the student's image as a researcher. The student will get credit for displaying the sources properly. The opposite, plagiarism, presents the information as though it were the student's own:

The great prairies of the world will soon dry up, and that includes America's, so a new water era has begun.

That sentence borrows too much. If in doubt, also cite the source and place it within its proper context. This issue will be further explained in Section 5d.

5b Identifying Bias in a Source

You will show integrity in your use of sources by identifying any bias expressed by a writer or implied by the political stance of a magazine. For example, if you are writing about federal aid to farmers, you will find different opinions in a farmers' magazine and a journal that promotes itself as a watchdog of federal spending. One is an advocate and the other a vocal opponent. You may quote them, but only if you identify them carefully. Let's examine the problem faced by one student. In researching articles on the world's water supply, Norman Berkowitz found an article of interest but positioned it with a description of the source, as shown in this note that carefully identifies the source of an alarmist attitude.

Earth First, which describes itself as a radical environmental journal, features articles by an editorial staff that uses pseudonyms, such as Sky, Jade, Wedge, and Sprig. In the article "The End of Lake Powell," Sprig says, "The Colorado River may soon be unable to provide for the 25 million people plumbed into its system" (25). The danger, however, is not limited to Lake Powell. Sprig adds, "This overconsumption of water, compounded with a regional drought cycle of 15 years, could mean that Lake Powell and every other reservoir in the upper Colorado River area will be without water" (24–25).

Be a responsible writer: Examine articles, especially those in magazines and on the Internet, for special interests, opinionated speculation, or an absence of credentials by the writer. Be wary of websites without an academic or government sponsor. Refer to Chapter 3, which lists the most reliable databases for evidence-based sources.

5c Honoring Property Rights

If you invent a new piece of equipment or a child's toy, you can get a patent that protects your invention. You now own it. If you own a company, you can register a symbol that serves as a trademark for the products produced. You own the trademark. In like manner, if you write a set of poems and publish them in a chap book, you own the poems. Others must seek your permission before they can reproduce the poems, just as others must not use your trademark or pay to produce your toy.

The principle behind the copyright law is relatively simple. Copyright begins at the time a creative work is recorded in some tangible form—a written document, a drawing, a tape recording. It does not depend upon a legal registration with the copyright office in Washington, DC, although published works are usually registered. The moment you express yourself creatively in any medium—on paper, on a canvas, electronically, and so on—that expression is your intellectual property. You have a vested interest in any profits made from the distribution of your work. For that reason, songwriters, cartoonists, fiction writers, and other artists guard their work and do not want it distributed without compensation.

In scholarly work there is seldom compensation, but there is certainly the need for recognition. We do that by providing in-text citations and bibliography entries. As a student you may use copyrighted material in your research paper under a doctrine of *fair use* as described in the U.S. Code, which says:

> The fair use of a copyrighted work . . . for purposes such as criticism, comment, news reporting, teaching (including multiple copies for classroom use), scholarship, or research is not an infringement of copyright.

Thus, as long as you borrow for educational purposes, such as a paper to be read by your instructor, you should not be concerned about violating the copyright law, as long as you provide documentation. However, if you decide to *publish* your research paper on a website, then new considerations come into play and you should seek the advice of your instructor.

5d   Avoiding Plagiarism

Plagiarism is offering the words or ideas of another person as one's own. Major violations, which can bring failure in the course or expulsion from school, are:

- The use of another student's work
- The purchase and submission of a "canned" research paper
- Copying passages into your paper without documentation
- Copying a key, well-worded phrase without documentation
- Placing specific ideas of others into your own words without documentation
- Inadequate or missing citations
- Missing quotation marks
- Incomplete or missing Works Cited entries

Whether deliberate or not, these instances all constitute forms of plagiarism. Closely related but not technically plagiarism is fabrication of information—that is, making up material off the top of your head. Some newspaper reporters have lost their jobs because of such fabrication.

There are a number of steps you can take to avoid plagiarism. First, develop personal notes full of your own ideas on a topic. Discover what you think and how you feel about the issue. Then, rather than copying sources one after another, express your own ideas at the beginning of paragraphs and then synthesize the ideas of others by using summary, paraphrase, and quotation. Rethink and reconsider ideas gathered by your reading, make meaningful connections, and when you refer to a specific source—as you inevitably will—give it credit.

Unintended plagiarism can result from student carelessness. Failing to enclose quoted material within quotation marks even though an in-text citation is given, or a paraphrase that never quite becomes paraphrase because too much of the original is left intact, are both examples of carelessness leading to plagiarism. In this area, instructors might step in and help the beginning researcher, for although these cases are not flagrant instances of plagiarism, these errors can mar an otherwise fine piece of research.

There is one safety net: Express clearly the name of your sources to let readers know the scope of your reading on the subject, as in this note:

> Commenting on the emotional role that music has on our
> lives, editor Marc Smirnoff makes this observation in *Oxford*

American: "The music that human beings rely on is essential
to them. We know which tunes to listen to when we need an
all-important lift (or when the party does) or when we want to
wallow in our sadness" (4).

Citations like this one help establish your credibility because they
make clear the sources that you have read and how your ideas blend
with the source.

CHECKLIST

Documenting Your Sources

- Let readers know when you begin borrowing from a
  source by introducing a quotation or paraphrase with
  the name of the authority.

- Enclose within quotation marks all quoted materials—
  keywords, phrases, sentences, or paragraphs.

- Make certain that paraphrased material has been rewrit-
  ten into your own style and language. The simple rear-
  rangement of sentence patterns is unacceptable.

- Provide specific in-text documentation for each borrowed item, but keep in mind that styles differ for MLA,
  APA, CMS, and CSE standards. These styles are explained
  in later chapters.

- Provide a bibliographic entry in the Works Cited section
  for every source cited in the paper.

Common Knowledge Exceptions

Common knowledge exceptions exist because you and your reader
will share the same perspectives on a subject. For example, if
you attend the University of Delaware, you need not cite the fact
that Wilmington is its largest city, or that Dover is the capital city.
Information of this sort requires *no* in-text citation because your local
audience will be knowledgeable:

The extended shoreline of Delaware provides one of the most
extensive series of national wildlife refuges in the eastern
United States. The state stretches from its northern border with
Pennsylvania to form a 100-mile border with Maryland to its
west and south. Its political center is Dover in the center of the

> state, but its commercial center is Wilmington, a great
> industrial city situated on Delaware Bay just below Philadelphia.

However, a writer in another place and time might need to cite the source of this information. Most writers would probably want to document this next passage.

> Early Indian tribes on the plains called themselves *Illiniwek*
> (which meant strong men), and French settlers pronounced the
> name *Illinois* (Angle 44).

Common factual information that one might find in an almanac, fact book, or dictionary need not be cited. Here is an example:

> President George H. W. Bush launched the Desert Storm attack
> in 1991 against Iraq and its leader Saddam Hussein with the
> support of allies and their troops from several nations. His
> son, President George W. Bush, launched a similar attack in
> 2003 against the same dictator and his army.

The passage needs no documentation, but the farther we move in history from that time and place, the more likely will be the need for documentation. Of course, provide a citation for analysis that goes beyond common facts.

C H E C K L I S T

Required Instances for Citing a Source

1. An original idea derived from a source, whether quoted or paraphrased. This next sentence requires an in-text citation and quotation marks around a key phrase.

> Genetic engineering, by which a child's body shape
> and intellectual ability is predetermined, raises for
> one source "memories of Nazi attempts in eugenics"
> (Riddell 19).

2. Your summary of original ideas by a source.

> Genetic engineering has been described as the
> rearrangement of the genetic structure in animals
> or in plants, which is a technique that takes a
> section of DNA and reattaches it to another section
> (Rosenthal 19–20).

3. Factual information that is not common knowledge within the context of the course.

> Genetic engineering has its risks: a nonpathogenic organism might be converted into a pathogenic one or an undesirable trait might develop as a result of a mistake (Madigan 51).

4. Any exact wording copied from a source.

> Kenneth Woodward asserts that genetic engineering is "a high stakes moral rumble that involves billions of dollars and affects the future" (68).

5e Sharing Credit in Collaborative Projects

Joint authorship is seldom a problem in collaborative writing, especially if each member of the project understands his or her role. Normally, all members of the team receive equal billing and credit. However, it might serve you well to predetermine certain issues with your peer group and the instructor:

- How will the project be judged and grades awarded?
- Will all members receive the same grade?
- Can a nonperformer be dismissed from the group?
- Should each member write a section of the work and everybody edit the whole?
- Should certain members write the draft and other members edit and load it onto a CD or onto the web?
- Can the group work together via e-mail rather than meeting frequently for group sessions?

Resolving such issues at the beginning of a project can go a long way toward eliminating entanglements and disagreements later.

5f Honoring and Crediting Sources in Online Classrooms

A rapidly growing trend in education is the web-based course or online course via e-mail. In general, you should follow the fair use doctrine of printed sources (see above, pages 63–67); that is, give proper credit and reproduce only limited portions of the original.

The rules are still emerging, and even faculty members are often in a quandary about how to transmit information back and forth. For educational purposes, the rules are pretty relaxed, and most publishers have made their texts or portions thereof available on the web. Plus, the copyrights of many works have expired, are now in the public domain, and are therefore free. In addition, many magazines and newspapers have made their online versions of articles available for free.

What you communicate back and forth with classmates and the instructor(s) has little privacy and even less protection. Rules are gradually emerging for electronic communication. In the meantime, abide by a few common sense principles:

1. Credit sources in your online communications just as you would in a printed research paper, with some variations:
   - The author, creator, or webmaster of the site
   - The title of the electronic article
   - The title of the website
   - The date of publication on the web
   - The date you accessed the site
   - The address (URL)
2. Download to your file only graphic images and text from sites that have specifically offered users the right to download them.
3. Non-free graphic images and text, especially an entire website, can be mentioned in your text, even paraphrased and quoted in a limited manner, but not downloaded into your file. Instead, link to them or point to them with URL addresses. In that way, your reader can go find the material and count it as a supplement to your text.
4. Seek permission if you download substantive blocks of material. See Section 5g if you wish to publish your work on the web.
5. If in doubt, consult by e-mail with your instructor, the moderator of a listserv, or the author of an Internet site.

5g   Seeking Permission to Publish Material on Your Website

You may wish to include your research papers on your personal website if you have one. However, the moment you do so, you are *publishing* the work and putting it into the public domain. That act carries responsibilities. In particular, the *fair use* doctrine of the U.S. Code refers to the personal educational purposes of your usage.

When you load borrowed images, text, music, or artwork onto the Internet, you are making that intellectual property available to everybody all over the world.

Short quotations, a few graphics, and a small quantity of illustrations to support your argument are examples of fair use. Permission will be needed, however, if the amount you borrow is substantial. The borrowing cannot affect the market for the original work, and you cannot misrepresent it in any way. The courts are still refining the law. For example, would your use of three *Doonesbury* comic strips be substantial? Yes, if you reproduce them in full. Would it affect the market for the comic strip? Perhaps. Follow these guidelines:

- Seek permission for copyrighted material that you publish within your web article. Most authors will grant permission at no charge. The problem is tracking down the copyright holder.
- If you make the attempt to get permission, and if your motive for using the material is *not for profit,* it is unlikely you will have any problem with the copyright owner. The owner would have to prove that your use of the image or text caused the owner financial harm.
- You may publish without permission works that are in the public domain, such as a section of Nathaniel Hawthorne's *The Scarlet Letter* or a speech by the president from the White House. In general, creative works enter the public domain after 75 years (the laws keep changing). Government papers are public domain.
- Document any and all sources that you feature on your website.
- If you provide hypertext links to other sites, you may need permission to do so.
- Be prepared for other persons to visit your website and even borrow from it. Decide beforehand how you will handle requests for use of your work, especially if it includes your creative efforts in poetry, art, music, or graphic design.

HINT: For information on the fair use laws, visit **http:// fairuse.stanford.edu/**.

6

Reading and Evaluating Sources

Clear Targets

The research paper assignment requires you to bring outside sources into your paper, so it only makes sense to choose the most reliable and well-written sources that you can find. This chapter cuts to the heart of the matter:

- Understanding the research assignment
- Identifying reliable sources
- Evaluating sources

In this age of electronic publications, finding sources worthy of citation in your paper can be a challenge. Your evaluation of source material should focus on the relevance of the source and how it conveys the idea that you are presenting. You must read and personally evaluate the sources for your own benefit as a writer and present the source material to your reader as validated and pertinent information. Also see pages 50–51 for guidelines on judging the value of Internet articles.

6a Selecting a Mix of Primary and Secondary Sources

Primary sources are the original words of an authority. Original source material can be found in novels, speeches, eyewitness accounts, interviews, letters, autobiographies, observation during field research, or the written results of empirical research. You should feel free to quote often from a primary source that has direct relevance to your discussion. For example, if you present a poem by Dylan Thomas, you should quote the poem.

Secondary sources are writings about the primary sources, about an author, or about somebody's accomplishments. This type of material is a commentary about original, primary information. Secondary sources include a report on a presidential speech, a review of new scientific findings, analysis of a poem, or a biography of a notable person. These evaluations, analyses, or interpretations provide ways of looking at original, primary sources. Following is a guide to sources for the major disciplines.

Guide to Academic Sources

Humanities

Primary sources in literature and the fine arts are novels, poems, and plays, as well as films, paintings, music, and sculptures. Your task is to examine, interpret, and evaluate these original works. Researchers in history need to look at speeches, documents written by historic figures, and some government documents.

Secondary sources in the humanities are evaluations in journal articles and books, critical reviews, biographies, and history books.

Field research in the humanities will require interviews with an artist or government official, letters, e-mail surveys, online discussion groups, or the archival study of manuscripts.

Social Sciences

Primary sources in education, political science, psychology, and other fields include speeches, writings by presidents and others, documents recorded in the *Congressional Record,* reports and statistics of government agencies and departments, and papers at your state's archival library.

Secondary sources include books and articles on social, political, and psychological issues; analyses and evaluations in journal articles; discussions of the business world in newspapers, magazines, and journals; and—in general—anything written about key personalities, events, products, and primary documents.

Field research is most important in the social sciences and will consist of case studies, findings from surveys and questionnaires, tests and test data, interviews, and observation. In business reports, field research consists of market testing, drawings and designs, industrial research, letters, and interviews.

Sciences

Primary sources in the various sciences consist of the words and theories of various scientists discussing natural phenomena or offering their views on scientific issues, such as the words of Charles Darwin or Stephen Hawking. At the same time, journal articles that report on empirical research are considered primary material because they are original in their testing of a hypothesis.

Secondary sources in the sciences are not abundant. They appear generally as review articles that discuss the testing and experiments by different scientists, for example, the review of four or five articles on gene mutation.

Field research and laboratory testing are crucial to the sciences and provide the results of experiments, discoveries, tests, and observations.

6b Identifying Reliable Sources

The inverted pyramid below presents a progression of sources from excellent down to less reliable. The chart does not ask you to ignore or dismiss items at the bottom, such as popular magazines or e-mail discussion groups, but it lets you know when to feel confident and when to be on guard about the validity of the source.

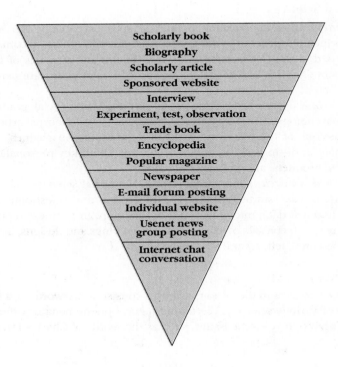

Scholarly book
Biography
Scholarly article
Sponsored website
Interview
Experiment, test, observation
Trade book
Encyclopedia
Popular magazine
Newspaper
E-mail forum posting
Individual website
Usenet news group posting
Internet chat conversation

Scholarly Book

Scholarly books, including textbooks, treat academic topics with in-depth discussions and careful documentation of the evidence. A college library is a repository for scholarly books—technical and scientific works, doctoral dissertations, publications of the university presses, and many textbooks. Scholarly books are subjected to careful review before publication, and they are published because they give the very best treatment on a subject. *Note:* In the sciences, books grow out-of-date quickly, so depend heavily upon monthly journals and updated Internet sites for current research.

Biography

The library's electronic catalog can help you find an appropriate biography from among the thousands available in such reference works as *Contemporary Authors* or *Dictionary of American Negro Biography*. You can also learn about a notable person on the Internet by using a search engine for the name of the person and carefully scanning the sites that are returned. Notable persons also have websites devoted to them.

You may need a biography for several reasons:

- To verify the standing and reputation of somebody you want to paraphrase or quote in your paper.
- To provide biographical details in your introduction. For example, the primary topic may be Carl Jung's psychological theories of the unconscious, but some information about Jung's career might also be appropriate in the paper.
- To discuss a creative writer's life in relation to his or her work. That is, Joyce Carol Oates's personal life may shed some light on your reading of her stories or novels.

Scholarly Articles

Scholarly articles are best found through one of the library's databases (see pages 20–25). The academic databases will take you to journal articles or articles at academically sponsored websites. You can be confident of the authenticity of journal articles because the authors document all sources, publish through university presses and academic organizations, and write for academic honor. Thus, a journal article about child abuse found in *Journal of Marriage and the Family* or through the PsyINFO database may be considered reliable. You may also find well-documented articles in respected periodicals, such as *The Atlantic, Scientific Review,* and *Discover.*

Major newspapers, such as the *New York Times, Atlanta Journal-Constitution,* and *Wall Street Journal,* also can be sources of valuable articles found in both printed and online editions.

Sponsored Website

The Internet supplies both excellent and dubious information. You must be careful when evaluating web materials. Chapter 3 explores research on the web. In addition to the "Evaluating Internet Sources" checklist on pages 50–51, you should ask yourself a few questions about any website information:

- Is it appropriate to my work?
- Does it reveal a serious and scholarly emphasis?
- Is it sponsored by a professional institution or organization?

Interview

Interviews with knowledgeable people provide excellent information for a research paper. Whether conducted in person, by telephone, or by e-mail, the interview brings a personal, expert perspective into your work. The key element, of course, is the experience of the person. For full details about conducting an interview, see pages 54–55.

Experiment, Test, or Observation

Gathering your own data for research is a staple in many fields, especially the sciences. An experiment will bring primary evidence into your paper as you explain your hypothesis, give the test results, and discuss the implications of your findings. For details on the format for a scientific investigation, see pages 58–59.

Trade Book

Good to Great: Why Some Companies Make the Leap . . . and Others Don't and *A Field Guide to Industrial Relations* are typical titles of nonfiction trade books to be found in bookstores, not in a college library, although public libraries often have some holdings in trade books. Designed for commercial consumption, trade books seldom treat in-depth a scholarly subject. Unlike scholarly books and textbooks, most manuscripts for trade books do not go through the rigors of peer review. For example, if your topic is "dieting" with a focus on "fad diets," you will find plenty of diet books at the local book store and numerous articles on commercial websites. However, serious discussions of fad diets backed by careful research will be found in journals or sponsored websites.

Encyclopedia

An encyclopedia, by design, contains brief surveys of every well-known person, event, place, and accomplishment. You may read an encyclopedia essay when you begin investigating a topic, but most instructors will prefer that you go beyond encyclopedias to cite from scholarly books and journal articles. However, specialized encyclopedias (see pages 26–28) often have in-depth articles by noted scholars.

Popular Magazine

Like a trade book, a magazine article seldom offers in-depth information and does not face critical review of a panel of experts. Thus, you must exercise caution when using a magazine as a source. In general, college libraries have magazines containing high-quality writing, so depend on your library's list of periodicals when judging quality.

Newspapers

Newspapers have reporters writing under the pressure of deadlines. They do not have as much time for the kind of careful research afforded writers of journal articles. On occasion, a newspaper will assign reporters to a series of articles on a complex topic, and such in-depth analyses have merit. The major print and online newspapers often hire highly qualified writers and columnists, so valuable articles can be found in these sources. Remember, however, that newspaper articles, like those in magazines and on the Internet, must be cautiously and critically evaluated.

E-mail Forum Posting

E-mail information via an e-mail forum established by the instructor for a course deserves consideration when it focuses on academic issues, such as "British Romantic literature," or more specifically "Shelley's poetry." In some cases, they originate for students in an online course, providing an avenue for sharing ideas. However, rather than search for quotable material from e-mail forums, use them as a sounding board to generate ideas and test them with other participants.

Individual Website

A person's home page, with its various links to other information, provides a publication medium for anybody who may or may not possess knowledge. You cannot avoid them, because they pop up on results lists of the search engines. You should approach them with caution. For example, one student, investigating the topic "fad diets," searched the web to find mostly home pages that described personal battles with weight loss or commercial sites that were blatant in their attempts to sell something. Caution becomes vital.

Social Media, Blogs, and Wikis

Although they can supply recent and up-to-date information, social media networks like Facebook, blogs, and wikis like Wikipedia, for example, are collaborative projects that cannot guarantee the expertise of their information. Most of these sources do not have a group moderator; hence, they post everything from expert data and testimony to opinions given by persons who are not experts in your field of study. Always be wary of these shared ventures, for they cannot guarantee the verifiability or expertise of their entries.

Internet Chat Conversations

Real-time Internet conversations have almost no value for academic research and are not legitimate sources for your paper. Seldom do you know the participants beyond their usernames, and the conversations rarely focus on scholarly issues.

Evaluating Sources

Confronted by several books and articles, many writers have trouble determining the value of material and the contribution it will make to their research paper. To save time, you need to be selective in your reading. To serve your reader, you need to cite carefully selected material that is pertinent to your argument. Avoid dumping huge blocks of quotation into your paper, because doing so results in the loss of your style and voice. As you select, evaluate, and use research materials, you must be concerned about the relevance, authority, accuracy, and currency of all sources that you cite.

Relevance

To determine how well an article or book fits the demands of your research, first skim the material. For a periodical or Internet article, examine the title, the abstract or introduction, and both the opening and closing paragraphs.

Authority

To test the authority of a source, examine the credentials of the author (usually found in a brief biographical profile or professional affiliation blurb) and the sponsoring institution, which is usually the publisher of a journal, such as the American Sociological Association, or the sponsors of a website, such as **http://www.ucla.edu/**. Look at the bibliography at the end of the article, for it signals the scholarly nature of the work and points you toward other material on your subject. Study the home page of an Internet article, if there is one. Prefer sites sponsored by universities and professional organizations. Take note of hypertext links to other sites whose quality may be determined by the domain tags .edu, .org, and .gov. Be wary of .com sites. See pages 50–51 for guidelines on judging the value of Internet articles.

Note: The **definitive edition** of a work is the most reliable version of a play, novel, or collection of poems because the definitive edition is one that the author supervised through the press. The way an author wanted to present the work can be found only in a definitive edition. Thus, electronic versions usually do not display the original author's page and type design, unless they are photocopies of the original, as with the JSTOR site (see page 23).

Accuracy

In the sciences, scholars talk about verification of an article, which means they can, if necessary, replicate the research and the findings described in the article. A scientific report must carefully detail the design of the work, as well as its methods, subjects, and procedures. A lab experiment, for example, should repeat previous findings to demonstrate accuracy. The writer should reveal the details of a control group, an experimental group, and the testing procedures. Any scientific report that does not establish research methods should not be cited.

Currency

Use recent sources for research in the sciences and social sciences. A psychology book may look valuable, but if its copyright date is 1955, the content probably is outdated and has been replaced by recent research and current developments. When reading a source, be certain that at least one date is listed. Electronic publications sometimes show the site has been updated or refreshed, but the article may carry an older date. On the Internet, check the date of print publication; it may be different from the web publication. As a general rule, use the most recent date for an article on the Internet, which means you could list as many as three dates—the year of the print publication, the most recent year of the Internet publication, and the date you accessed the material.

7

Organizing Ideas and Setting Goals

Clear Targets

Each research assignment demands its own approach depending on the field of study. The organizational models in this chapter will help you organize your notes, photocopies, and downloaded files:

- Using the correct academic model (paradigm)
- Using your thesis to control the outline
- Writing an outline

Because research is often haphazard, you will need to organize the information that you have gathered to serve your specific needs. The structure of your project becomes clear only when you organize your research materials into a proposal, a list of ideas, a set of questions, or a rough outline. In most cases, the design of your study should match an appropriate organizational model, sometimes called a **paradigm**, which means "an example that serves as a pattern or model." By following an academic model, you can ensure that your research project will have the correct design to meet the demands of the assignment.

7a Creating Outlines Using Academic Models (Paradigms)

A traditional outline, because it is content specific, is useful for only one paper, while an academic pattern, such as those shown below, governs all papers within a certain design. For example, a general, all-purpose model gives a plan for almost any research topic.

A General, All-Purpose Model

If you are uncertain about your assignment, start with this basic model and expand it with your material to make it a detailed outline. It offers plenty of leeway. Readers, including your instructor, are accustomed to this sequence for research papers.

- Identify the subject in the *introduction*. Explain the problem, provide background information, and give a clear thesis statement.
- Analyze the subject in the *body* of the paper. You can compare, analyze, give evidence, trace historical events, and handle other matters.
- Discuss your findings in the *conclusion*. You can challenge an assumption, interpret the findings, provide solutions, or reaffirm your thesis.

The specific design of any model is based on the nature of the assignment and the discipline for which you are writing. Each of the following forms is explained below.

Model for the Interpretation of Literature and Other Creative Works

If you plan to interpret a musical, artistic, or literary work, such as an opera, a set of paintings, or a novel, adjust this next model to your subject and purpose and build it, with your factual data, into a working outline:

Introduction
    Identify the work.
    Give a brief summary in one sentence.
    Provide background information that relates to the thesis.
    Offer biographical facts about the artist that relate to the specific issues.
    Quote and paraphrase authorities to establish the scholarly traditions.
    Write a thesis sentence that establishes your particular views of the literary work.
Body
    Provide evaluative analysis divided by imagery, theme, design, use of color, character development, structure, symbolism, narration, language, musical themes, and so forth.

Conclusion

Keep a fundamental focus on the artist of the work, not just the elements of analysis as explained in the body.

Offer a conclusion that explores the contributions of the artist in accordance with your thesis sentence.

Model for the Analysis of History

If you are writing a historical or political science paper that analyzes events and their causes and consequences, your paper should conform in general to the following plan. Flesh it out with the notes in your research journal to make it a working outline for drafting your paper.

Introduction

Identify the event.

Provide the background leading up to the event.

Offer quotations and paraphrases from experts.

Give the thesis sentence.

Body

Analyze the background leading up to the event.

Trace events from one historic episode to another.

Offer a chronological sequence that explains how one event relates directly to the next.

Cite authorities who have also investigated this event in history.

Conclusion

Reaffirm your thesis.

Discuss the consequences of this event.

Model for Advancing Philosophical and Religious Ideas

If the assignment is to defend or analyze a topic from the history of ideas, use this next design, but adjust it as necessary. Make it your working outline by writing sentences and even paragraphs for each item in the model.

Introduction

Establish the idea or question.

Trace its history.

Discuss its significance.

Introduce experts who have addressed the idea.

Provide a thesis sentence that presents your approach to the issue(s), from a fresh perspective if at all possible.

Body
> Evaluate the issues surrounding the concept.
> Develop a past-to-present examination of theories.
> Compare and analyze the details and minor issues.
> Cite experts who have addressed this idea.

Conclusion
> Advance and defend your thesis as it grows out of evidence about the idea.
> Close with an effective quotation from a noted person.

Model for the Review of a Performance

If the assignment asks you to review a musical, artistic, or literary performance, such as an opera, a set of paintings, a reading, a drama, or a theatrical performance, adjust this next paradigm to your subject and purpose. *Note:* The review differs from the interpretation (see page 79) by its focus on evaluation rather than on analysis.

Introduction
> Identify the work.
> Give a brief summary in one sentence.
> Provide background information or history of the work.
> Offer biographical facts about the artist that relate to the specific issues.
> Quote and paraphrase authorities to establish the scholarly traditions that relate to this work and the performance.
> Write a thesis sentence that establishes your judgment about the performance.

Body
> Offer an evaluation as based upon a predetermined set of criteria. Judge a drama by its staging and acting, music by its quality of voice and instruments, art by its design, literature by its themes, and so forth.

Conclusion
> Keep a fundamental focus on the performance, the performers, and the artist of the work.
> Offer a judgment, as based on the criteria given in the body.

Model for Advancing Your Ideas and Theories

If you want to advance a social or legal theory in your paper, use this next design, but adjust it to eliminate some items and add new elements as necessary. Build this model into a working outline by assigning your notes, photocopies, and downloaded files to a specific line of the model.

Introduction
> Establish the theory, problem, or question.
> Discuss its significance.
> Provide the necessary background information.
> Introduce experts who have addressed the problem.
> Provide a thesis sentence that relates the problem to a fresh perspective.

Body
> Evaluate the issues involved in the problem.
> Develop a chronological examination.
> Compare and analyze the details and minor issues.
> Cite experts who have addressed the same problem.

Conclusion
> Advance and defend your theory.
> Discuss the implications of your findings.
> Offer directives or a plan of action.
> Suggest additional research that might be appropriate.

Model for Argument and Persuasion Papers

If you write persuasively or argue from a set position, your paper should conform in general to this next paradigm. Select the elements that fit your design, begin to elaborate on them, and gradually build a frame for your paper.

Introduction
> Establish clearly the problem or controversy that your paper will examine.
> Summarize the issues.
> Define key terminology.
> Make concessions on some points of the argument.
> Use quotations and paraphrases to explore the controversy.
> Provide background information.
> Write a thesis to establish your position.

Body
> Develop arguments to defend one side of the subject.
> Analyze the issues, both pro and con.
> Give evidence from the sources, including quotations from the scholarship as appropriate.

Conclusion
> Expand your thesis into a conclusion to demonstrate that your position has been formulated logically through careful analysis and discussion of the issues.

Model for a Comparative Study

A comparative study requires that you examine two schools of thought, two issues, two works, or the positions taken by two persons. It explores similarities and differences, generally using one of three arrangements for the body of the paper. As you embellish the model, you will gradually build your working outline.

Introduction
> Establish A.
> Establish B.
> Briefly compare the two.
> Introduce the central issues.
> Cite source materials on the subjects.
> Present your thesis.

Body (choose one)

Examine A	Compare A & B	Issue 1: Discuss A & B
Examine B	Contrast A & B	Issue 2: Discuss A & B
Compare and contrast A & B	Discuss the central issues	Issue 3: Discuss A & B

Conclusion
> Discuss the significant issues.
> Write a conclusion that ranks one over the other, or write a conclusion that rates the respective genius of each side.

Model for a Laboratory Investigation or Field Report

This model is rigid with little flexibility. Instructors will expect your report to remain tightly focused on each of these items.

Introduction
> Provide the title, the experiment number, and the date.
> Describe the experiment.
> List any literature consulted.
> Objectively describe what it is that you hope to accomplish.

Method
> Explain the procedures used to reproduce an experiment.

Explain the design of the test.

Identify any tools or apparatus used.

Identify any variables that affected your research (weather conditions, temperatures, and so on).

Results

Give your findings, including statistical data.

Discussion

Provide your interpretation of the data.

Discuss any implications to be drawn from the research.

Comment on what you learned by the experiment (optional).

Model for Scientific Analysis

In this situation, you are working with the literature on a scientific issue, so you have more flexibility than with a report on a lab experiment.

Introduction

Identify the scientific issue or problem and state your hypothesis.

Explore the history of the topic.

Cite the literature that pertains to the topic.

Explain the purpose of the examination and its possible implications.

Body

Classify the issues.

Analyze, define, and compare each aspect of the topic.

Offer cause/effect explanations.

Make a detailed inquiry into all relevant issues.

Conclusion

Explain the current findings of scientific studies related to your topic.

Advance your reasons for continued research.

Suggest possible findings.

Discuss the implications of your analysis.

Model for a Report of Empirical Research

This pattern is similar to the one for a laboratory investigation, so follow it closely to fulfill all the required items.

Introduction

Present the point of your study.

State the hypothesis and how it relates to the problem.

Provide the theoretical implications.

Explain the manner in which your study relates to previously published work.

Method

Describe the subject (what was tested, who participated, whether the participants were human or animal, and where the field work was accomplished).

Describe the apparatus, to explain your equipment and how you used it.

Summarize the procedure and the execution of each stage of your work.

Results

Summarize the data you collected.

Provide statistical treatment of your findings with tables, graphs, and charts.

Include findings that conflict with your hypothesis.

Discuss the implications of your work.

Evaluate the data and its relevance to the hypothesis.

Interpret the findings as necessary.

Discuss the implications of the findings.

Qualify the results and limit them to your specific study.

Make inferences from the results.

Suggest areas worthy of additional research.

7b Using Your Thesis to Control the Outline

After you have selected an academic pattern appropriate to your assignment, you should use your thesis statement (or hypothesis) to set the tone and direction of your paper. Notice in the following examples how variations in the thesis can affect the arrangement of the paper.

Argument

THESIS: Misunderstandings about organ donation distort reality and set serious limits on the availability of organs for those persons? who need an eye, a liver, or a healthy heart.

ARGUMENT 1. Many myths mislead people into believing that donation is unethical.

ARGUMENT 2.	Some fear that as a patient they might be put down early.
ARGUMENT 3.	Religious views sometimes get in the way of donation.

This preliminary outline gives this writer three categories for an analysis of the issues.

Cause and Effect

THESIS:	Television can have positive effects on a child's language development.
CONSEQUENCE 1.	Television introduces new words.
CONSEQUENCE 2.	Television reinforces word usage and proper syntax.
CONSEQUENCE 3.	Literary classics come alive on television.
CONSEQUENCE 4.	Television exposes children to the subtle rhythms and musical effects of accomplished speakers.

Evaluation

THESIS:	The architectural drawing for the university's new student center shows the design is not friendly to people who are handicapped.
EVALUATION 1.	The common areas seem cramped and narrow, with few open areas in which students can cluster.
EVALUATION 2.	Steps and stairs seem all too common in the design.
EVALUATION 3.	Only one elevator appears in the plans when three would be fair and equitable.
EVALUATION 4.	Only the first-floor restrooms offer universal access.
EVALUATION 5.	The parking spaces designated for people with physical handicaps are located at an entrance with steps, not a ramp.

The outline evolves from a thesis statement that invites evaluation of an architectural plan.

Comparison

THESIS:	Discipline often involves punishment, but child abuse adds another element: the gratification of the adult.

COMPARISON 1:	A spanking has the interest of the child at heart, but a beating or a caning has no redeeming value.
COMPARISON 2:	Time-outs remind the child that relationships are important and to be cherished, but lock-outs in a closet only promote hysteria and fear.
COMPARISON 3:	The parent's ego and selfish interests often take precedence over the welfare of the child or children.

This outline provides a pattern of comparison by which to judge the relative differences between punishment of a child and child abuse.

7c Writing an Outline

Not all papers require a complete, formal outline, nor do all researchers need one. A short research paper can be created from key words, a list of issues, a rough outline, and a first draft. Creating a formal outline can be worthwhile, however, for it fleshes out the academic pattern you have selected (see 7a) by classifying the issues of your study into clear, logical categories with main headings and one or more levels of subheadings.

A formal outline is not rigid and inflexible; you may, and should, modify it while writing and revising. In every case, treat an outline or organizational chart as a tool. Like an architect's blueprint, it should contribute to, not inhibit, the construction of a finished product. You may wish to experiment with the "outline" feature of your software, which allows you to view the paper at various levels of detail and to highlight and "drop" the essay into a different organization.

Topic Outline

Build a topic outline of balanced phrases. You can use noun phrases ("the rods of the retina"), gerund phrases ("sensing dim light with retina rods"), or infinitive phrases ("to sense dim light with retina rods"). No matter which grammatical format you choose, follow it consistently throughout the outline. One student used noun phrases to outline her scientific analysis:

    I. Diabetes defined
        A. A disease without control
            1. A disorder of the metabolism
            2. The search for a cure

B. Types of diabetes
  1. Type 1, juvenile diabetes
  2. Type 2, adult onset diabetes

II. Health complications
  A. The problem of hyperglycemia
    1. Signs and symptoms of the problem
    2. Lack of insulin
  B. The conflict of the kidneys and the liver
    1. Effects of ketoacidosis
    2. Effects of arteriosclerosis

III. Proper care and control
  A. Blood sugar monitoring
    1. Daily monitoring at home
    2. Hemoglobin test at a laboratory
  B. Medication for diabetes
    1. Insulin injections
    2. Hypoglycemia agents
  C. Exercise programs
    1. Walking
    2. Swimming
    3. Aerobic workouts
  D. Diet and meal planning
    1. Exchange plan
    2. Carbohydrate counting

IV. Conclusion: Balance of all the factors

Sentence Outline

In contrast to an outline with phrases, you may use full sentences for each heading and subheading. Using sentences has two advantages over the topic outline: (1) many entries in a sentence outline can serve as topic sentences for paragraphs, thereby accelerating the writing process, and (2) the subject-verb pattern establishes the logical direction of your thinking (for example, the phrase *Vocabulary development* becomes *Television viewing can improve a child's vocabulary*). Note below a brief portion of one student's sentence outline.

I. Organ and tissue donation is the gift of life.
  A. Organs that can be successfully transplanted include the heart, lungs, liver, kidneys, and pancreas.

B. Tissues that can be transplanted successfully include bone, corneas, skin, heart valves, veins, cartilage, and other connective tissues.

C. The process of becoming a donor is easy.

D. Many people receive organ and tissue transplants each year, but still many people die because they did not receive the needed transplant.

8

Writing Effective Notes

Clear Targets

Note taking is the heart of research. If you write high-quality notes, they may need only minor editing to fit into the appropriate places in your first draft. Prepare yourself to write different types of notes—quotations for well-phrased passages by authorities but also paraphrased or summarized notes to maintain your voice. This chapter explains the following types of notes:

- *Personal notes* that express your own ideas or record field research
- *Quotation notes* that preserve any distinguished syntax of an authority
- *Paraphrase notes* that interpret and restate what the authority has said
- *Summary notes* that capture in capsule form a writer's ideas
- *Field notes* that record interviews, tabulate questionnaires, and maintain records of laboratory experiments and other types of field research

Honoring the Conventions of Research Style

Your note taking will be more effective from the start if you practice the conventions of style for citing a source within your text, as advocated by MLA, APA, CSE, or CMS and as shown briefly below (see pages 110–112 for a full explanation of the differences among MLA, APA, CMS, and CSE styles).

MLA: Lawrence Smith states, "The suicidal teen causes severe damage to the psychological condition of peers" (34).

APA: Smith (2012) stated, "The suicidal teen causes severe damage to the psychological condition of peers" (p. 34).

CMS footnote: Lawrence Smith explains, "The suicidal teen causes severe damage to the psychological condition of peers."[3]

CSE number: Smith (4) said, "The suicidal teen causes severe damage to the psychological condition of peers."

The MLA style is the default style displayed throughout this chapter.

C H E C K L I S T

Writing Effective Notes

1. Whether you are using a research journal or your computer for Word documents, create a separate, labeled file within a project folder for each note topic or source. Keep notes and downloaded materials in the files.

2. Include the name, year, and page of all sources in order to prepare for creating in-text citations.

3. Label each file (for example, "objectivity on television").

4. Write a full note in well-developed sentences to speed the writing of your first draft.

5. Keep everything (photocopy, scribbled note) in order to authenticate dates, page numbers, or full names.

6. Label your personal notes with "my idea" or "personal note" to distinguish them from the sources.

8a   Writing Personal Notes

The content of a research paper is an expression of your own ideas as supported by scholarly evidence. It is not a collection of ideas transmitted by experts in books and articles. Readers are primarily interested in *your* thesis statement, *your* topic sentences, and *your* personal view of the issues. Therefore, during your research, record your thoughts on the issues by writing plenty of personal notes in your research journal and computer files. Personal notes are essential because they allow you to record your discoveries, reflect on the findings, make connections, and identify the prevailing views and patterns of thought. Remember two standards: (1) the idea written into the file is yours, and (2) the file is labeled with "my idea," "mine," or "personal thought" to distinguish it from information borrowed from a source. Here is an example:

> Personal thought
>
> For me, organ donation might be a gift of life, so I have signed my donor card. At least a part of me will continue to live if an accident claims my life. My boyfriend says I'm gruesome, but I consider it practical. Besides, he might be the one who benefits, and then what will he say?

8b Writing Direct Quotation Notes

Quotation notes are essential because they allow you to capture the authoritative voices of the experts on the topic, feature well-phrased statements, offer conflicting points of view, and share the literature on the topic with your readers. Follow these basic conventions.

1. Select material that is important and well phrased, not something trivial or something that is common knowledge. NOT "John F. Kennedy was a Democrat from Massachusetts" (Rupert 233) but this:

   > "John F. Kennedy's Peace Corps left a legacy of lasting compassion for the downtrodden"(Rupert 233).

2. Use quotation marks around the quoted material in your notes, working draft, and final manuscript. Do not copy or download the words of a source into your paper in such a way that readers will think that *you* wrote the material.

3. Use the exact words of the source.

4. Provide an appropriate in-text citation, as shown by this note:

   > Griffiths, Kilman, and Frost suggest that the killing of architect Stanford White in 1904 was "the beginning of the most bitterly savage century known to mankind" (113). Murder, wars, and human atrocities were the "sad vestiges" of an era that had great promise.

5. The parenthetical citation goes *outside* the final quotation mark but *inside* the period for quotations run on within your sentence. Block quotations require a different setup (see pages 94–95).

6. Quote key sentences and short passages, not entire paragraphs. Find the essential statement and feature it; do not force your reader to read a long quoted passage that has only one statement relevant to your point. Make the essential idea a part of your sentence, as shown here:

Many Americans, trying to mend their past eating habits, adopt functional foods as an essential step toward a more health-conscious future. Balthrop says this group of believers spends "an estimated $29 billion a year" on functional foods (6).

7. Quote from both primary sources (the original words by a writer or speaker) and secondary sources (the comments after the fact about original works). The two types are discussed immediately below.

Quoting the Primary Sources

Quote from primary sources for four specific reasons:

- To draw on the wisdom of the original author
- To let readers hear the precise words of the original author
- To copy exact lines of poetry and drama
- To reproduce graphs, charts, and statistical data

Cite poetry, fiction, drama, letters, and interviews. In other cases, you may want to quote liberally from a presidential speech, cite the words of a businessman, or reproduce original data.

Quoting the Secondary Sources

Quote from secondary sources for three specific reasons:

- To display excellence in ideas and expression by experts on the topic
- To explain complex material
- To set up a statement of your own, especially if it spins off, adds to, or takes exception to the source as quoted

The overuse of direct quotation from secondary sources indicates that either you (1) did not have a clear focus and copied verbatim just about everything related to the subject, or (2) had inadequate evidence and used numerous quotations as padding. Therefore, limit quotations from secondary sources by using only a phrase or a sentence:

Reginald Herman says the geographical changes in Russia require "intensive political analysis" (15).

If you quote an entire sentence, make the quotation a direct object. It tells *what* the authority says.

In response to the changes in Russia, one critic notes, "The American government must exercise caution and conduct intensive political analysis" (15).

8c   Writing Paraphrased Notes

A paraphrase requires you to restate in your own words the thought, meaning, and attitude of someone else. Your interpretation acts as a bridge between the source and the reader as you capture the wisdom of the source in approximately the same number of words. Use paraphrase to maintain your voice or style in the paper, to avoid an endless string of direct quotations, and to interpret the source as you rewrite it. Keep in mind these five rules for paraphrasing a source:

1. Rewrite the original in about the same number of words.
2. Provide an in-text citation to the source (the author and page number in MLA style).
3. Retain exceptional words and phrases from the original by enclosing them within quotation marks.
4. Preserve the tone of the original by suggesting moods of satire, anger, humor, doubt, and so on. Show the author's attitude with appropriate verbs: "Omar Tavares condemns . . . defends . . . argues . . . explains . . . observes . . . defines."
5. Put the original aside while paraphrasing to avoid copying word for word. Compare the finished paraphrase with the original source to be certain that the paraphrase truly rewrites the original and that it uses quotation marks with any phrasing or key words retained from the original.

HINT: When instructors see an in-text citation but no quotations marks, they will assume that you are paraphrasing, not quoting. Be sure that their assumption is true.

Here are examples that show the differences between a quotation note and a paraphrased one:

Quotation:

Hein explains heredity in this way: "Except for identical twins, each person's heredity is unique" (294).

Paraphrase:

One source explains that heredity is special and distinct for
each of us, unless a person is one of identical twins (Hein 294).

Quotation (block indent if four lines or more):

Hein explains the phenomenon in this way:

> Since only half of each parent's chromosomes are transmitted
> to a child and since this half represents a chance selection
> of those the child could inherit, only twins that develop
> from a single fertilized egg that splits in two have identical
> chromosomes. (294)

Paraphrase:

Hein specifies that twins have identical chromosomes because they
grow from one egg that divides after it has been fertilized. He
affirms that most brothers and sisters differ because of the "chance
selection" of chromosomes transmitted by each parent (294).

As shown in the example immediately above, place any key
wording of the source within quotation marks.

8d Writing Summary Notes

A summary of a source captures in just a few words the ideas of an
entire paragraph, section, or chapter. It may be a rough sketch of the
source or a polished note. Store each summary in your project folder
with its own file name. Use a summary for these reasons:

- To review an article or book
- To annotate a bibliography entry
- To provide a plot summary
- To create an abstract

Success with the summary requires you do the following:

1. Condense the original content with precision and directness.
   Reduce a long paragraph into a sentence, tighten an article into
   a brief paragraph, and summarize a book into a page.
2. Preserve the tone of the original. If the original is serious, suggest that tone in the summary. In the same way, retain moods of
   doubt, skepticism, optimism, and so forth.
3. Write the summary in your own language; however, retain exceptional phrases from the original, enclosing them in quotation marks.
4. Provide documentation.

Using the Summary to Review Briefly an Article or Book

Note this example that reviews two entire articles:

> Alec Twobears has two closely related articles on this
> subject, and both, one in 2009 and another in 2010,
> are about the failure of the United States to follow through
> with the treaties it signed with the Indian nations of North
> America. He opens both with "No treaty is a good treaty!" He
> signals clearly the absence of trust by Native Americans toward
> the government in Washington, DC.

To see more summaries of this type, presented in a review of the literature, see pages 100–108.

Using the Summary to Write an Annotated Bibliography

An annotation offers a brief explanation or critical commentary on an article or book. Thus, an annotated bibliography is one that cites a source followed immediately by the annotation, as shown here in MLA style.

> "Top Ten Myths About Donation and Transplantation."
>   TransWeb Webcast. 4 Feb. 2010. Web. 21 Feb. 2012. This
>   site dispels the many myths surrounding organ donation,
>   showing that selling organs is illegal, that matching donor
>   and recipient is highly complicated, and secret back room
>   operations are almost impossible.

See pages 98–100 to view more annotated bibliography entries.

Using the Summary in a Plot Summary Note

In just a few sentences, a summary can describe a novel, short story, drama, or similar literary work, as shown by this next note:

> Great Expectations by Dickens describes young Pip, who inherits
> money and can live the life of a gentleman. But he discovers
> that his "great expectations" have come from a criminal. With
> that knowledge his attitude changes from one of vanity to one of
> compassion.

Using the Summary to Create an Abstract

An abstract is a brief description that appears at the beginning of an article to summarize the contents. Usually, it is written by the article's author, and it helps readers make decisions about reading the entire article. You can find entire volumes devoted to abstracts, such as *Psychological Abstracts* or *Abstracts of English Studies*. An abstract is required for most papers in the social and natural sciences. Here is a sample from one student's paper:

Abstract

Functional foods, products that provide benefits beyond basic nutrition, are adding billions to the nation's economy each year. Functional foods are suspected to be a form of preventive medicine. Consumers hope that functional foods can calm some of their medical anxieties, while researchers believe that functional foods may lower health care costs. The paper identifies several functional foods, locates the components that make them work, and explains the role that each plays on the body.

Writing Notes from Field Research

For some research projects, you will be expected to conduct field research. This work may require you record your notes on charts, on cards, on notepads, on laboratory notebooks, in a research journal, or on the computer. **Interviews** require careful note taking during the session and dutiful transcription of those notes to your draft. A tape recorder can serve as a backup to your note taking. A **questionnaire** produces valuable data for developing notes and graphs and charts for your research paper.

The procedures and findings of **experiments, tests, and measurements** serve as your notes for the "method" and "results" section of the report. Here is an example of one student's laboratory notebook containing a passage that he might transfer to the "procedures" section of his paper:

First, 25.0 ml of a vinegar sample was delivered to a 50-ml volumetric flask, with a 25-ml pipet, and diluted to the mark with distilled water. It was mixed thoroughly and 50-ml aliquot were emptied into three 250-ml conical flasks, with a 25 ml pipet, 50 ml of distilled water, and two drops of phenolphthalein were added to each of the flasks. The samples were then titrated with a .345 M NaOH solution until the first permanent pink color.

8f   Using Your Notes to Write an Annotated Bibliography

Writing an annotated bibliography may appear as busywork, but it helps you evaluate the strength and nature of your sources. The annotated bibliography that follows is written in MLA style. An *annotation* is a summary of the contents of a book or article. A *bibliography* is a list of sources on a selected topic. Thus, an annotated bibliography does two important things: (1) it is a bibliographic list of a selection of sources, and (2) it summarizes the contents of each book or article.

The annotated bibliography below provides a summary of a few sources on the issues of tanning, tanning beds, lotions, and the dangers of skin cancer.

Delgado 1

Norman Delgado

Dr. Pasch

English 2120

24 January 2012

Each entry gives full bibliographic information on the source—author, title, and publication data—as well as a brief description of the article or book.

Annotated Bibliography

"Better Laws Needed to Curb Teen Tanning Bed Use: Report." St. Louis Children's Hospital. 17 Mar. 2011. Web. 17 Jan. 2012. This article from the St. Louis Children's Hospital calls for more stringent laws regarding indoor tanning by adolescents. Current laws, most of which involve parental consent requirements, are not working. "The high rate of indoor tanning by older adolescent girls suggests that better laws are needed, preferably in the form of bans for those younger than 18 years as recommended by the World Health Organization. Parents who influence their adolescents' indoor tanning behavior both by modeling this behavior themselves and by granting

Delgado 2

their permission for their adolescents to tan could play an important role in lowering their adolescents' melanoma risk."

Conforth, Tracee. "Indoor Tanning Booths: Are Indoor Tanning Booths Safe?" Women's Health. 9 Sept. 2009. Web. 15 Jan. 2012. This site raises the central question of whether tanning booths are less dangerous than tans from the sun. Most lay people agree that solar radiation is damaging to our skin. The fact is that some who tan not only accept, but expect skin to pass through these damaging changes. For these individuals, a deep, golden glow offsets the risk of skin cancer.

Mayer, Joni A., et al. "Adolescents' Use of Indoor Tanning: A Large-Scale Evaluation of Psychosocial, Environmental, and Policy-Level Correlates." *American Journal of Public Health* 101 (2011): 930–38. Print. This study surveyed 6,000 teenagers ages 14 to 17 over a one-year period about their tanning habits. Researchers found that 17.1 percent of girls and 3.2 percent of boys used indoor tanning within that year. The study also showed that the same number of teens went tanning in states with laws that have age restrictions or require parental consent. Older teenage girls hit the tanning booths most often.

Narayan, Adi. "Cancer and Teen Tanning: Where's the Regulation?" *Time Magazine Online*. 12 Oct. 2009. Web. 17 Jan. 2012. Narayan warns that "the UV light from tanning beds is no different from sunlight— exposure to either one raises the risk of skin cancer." Citing numerous studies, the writer explains that tanning salons are not well regulated, so the amount of exposure can be really dangerous. The writer also explains how skin type affects tanning and the dangers of cancer.

Delgado 3

Schwartz, Joan. "Melanoma an equal-opportunity killer." *Research Briefs*. Boston U. 15 May 2003. Web. 18 Jan. 2012. This article cites Dr. Marie-France Demierre, a professor of dermatology, who laments the use of tanning beds by young women. In truth, women are joining men in contracting and dying of melanoma, in great part because of tanning beds. The article warns against addiction to tanning beds as well as sun worship.

"Skin Care for Your Type and Tone." Harvard Medical School. 7 Dec. 2009. Web. 18 Jan. 2012. This site features Harvard Medical School's Consumer Health Information. In this article, information is given about the main types of skin tone as well as advice about tanning, including the use of sunscreen of SPF 15 or higher, use of suntan lotions, the effects of the sun, and the dangers of skin cancer.

"Sunny Days." *Health Watch*. The U of Texas Southwestern Medical Center at Dallas. 2011. Web. 21 Jan. 2012. This article warns against sun worship and skipping sunscreen. Experts suggest more public education and warnings, for tanning damages the structure of the skin and promotes sagging skin and wrinkles in later life. Dr. Sarah Weitzul, a UT Southwestern dermatologist, says proper sunscreen use is the key to saving your skin from the sun.

8g Using Your Notes to Write a Review of the Literature

A review of literature presents a set of summaries in essay form. It has two purposes:

1. It helps you investigate the topic because it forces you to examine and then evaluate how each source addresses the problem.

2. It organizes and classifies the sources in some reasonable manner for the benefit of the reader.

Thus, you should relate each source to your central subject, and you should group the sources according to their support of your thesis. For example, the brief review that follows explores the literature on the subject of gender communication. It classifies the sources under a progression of headings: the issues, the causes (both environmental and biological), the consequences for both men and women, and possible solutions.

You also will need to arrange the sources according to your selected categories or to fit your preliminary outline. Sometimes it might be as simple as grouping those sources that favor a course of action and those that oppose it. In other cases you may need to summarize sources that examine different characters or elements.

Like Kaci Holz in the paper below, you may wish to use headings that identify your various sections.

Holz 1

Kaci Holz
Dr. Bekus
English 1020
April 23, 2012

Gender Communication: A Review of the Literature

Several theories exist about different male and female communication styles. These ideas have been categorized below to establish the issues, shows causes for communication failures, the consequences for both men and women, and suggestions for possible solutions.

The review of literature is an essay on the articles and books that address the writer's topic.

The Issues

Deborah Tannen, Ph.D., is a professor of sociolinguistics at Georgetown University. In her book *You Just Don't Understand: Men and Women in Conversation*, she claims there are basic gender patterns or stereotypes that can be found. Tannen says that men participate in conversations to establish "a hierarchical social order,"

The writer uses the sources to establish the issues.

Holz 2

while women most often participate in conversations to establish "a network of connections" (Tannen, *Don't Understand* 24–25). She distinguishes between the way women use "rapport-talk" and the way men use "report-talk" (74).

In similar fashion, Susan Basow and Kimberly Rubenfeld in "'Troubles Talk': Effects of Gender and Gender Typing," explore in detail the sex roles and how they determine and often control the speech of each gender. They notice that "women may engage in 'troubles talk' to enhance communication; men may avoid such talk to enhance autonomy and dominance (186).

In addition, Kawa Patel asserts that men and women "use conversation for quite different purposes." He provides a "no" answer to the question in his title, "Do Men and Women Speak the Same Language?" He claims that women converse to develop and maintain connections, while men converse to claim their position in the hierarchy they see around them. Patel asserts that women are less likely to speak publicly than are men because women often perceive such speaking as putting oneself on display. A man, on the other hand, is usually comfortable with speaking publicly because that is how he establishes his status among others (Patel).

Similarly, masculine people are "less likely than androgynous individuals to feel grateful for advice" (Basow and Rubenfeld 186).

Julia T. Wood's book *Gendered Lives* claims that "male communication is characterized by assertion, independence, competitiveness, and confidence [while] female communication is characterized by deference, inclusivity, collaboration, and cooperation" (440). This list of differences describes why men and women have such opposing communication styles.

Holz 3

In another book, Tannen addresses the issue that boys, or men, "are more likely to take an oppositional stance toward other people and the world" and "are more likely to find opposition entertaining—to enjoy watching a good fight, or having one" (Tannen, *Argument* 166). Girls try to avoid fights.

Causes

Two different theories suggest causes for gender differences—the environment and biology.

<u>Environmental Causes</u>. Tammy James and Bethan Cinelli mention, "The way men and women are raised contributes to differences in conversation and communication . . ." (41).

> The writer now uses the sources to explain the causes for communication failures.

Another author, Susan Witt, in "Parental Influence on Children's Socialization to Gender Roles," discusses the various findings that support the idea that parents have a great influence on their children during the development of their self-concept. She states, "Children learn at a very early age what it means to be a boy or a girl in our society" (253). She says that parents "[dress] infants in gender-specific colors, [give] gender-differentiated toys, and [expect] different behavior from boys and girls" (Witt 254).

Patel notices a cultural gap, defining culture as "shared meaning." He goes on to comment that problems come about because one spouse enters marriage with a different set of "shared meanings" than the other. The cultural gap affects the children. Patel also talks about the "Battle of the Sexes" as seen in conflict between men and women. Reverting back to his "childhood gender pattern" theory, Patel claims, "Men, who grew up in a hierarchical environment, are accustomed to conflict. Women,

Holz 4

concerned more with relationship and connection, prefer the role of peacemaker."

Like Patel, Deborah Tannen also addresses the fact that men and women often come from different worlds and different influences. She says, "Even if they grow up in the same neighborhood, on the same block, or in the same house, girls and boys grow up in different worlds of words" (Tannen, *Don't Understand* 43).

<u>Biological Causes</u>. Though Tannen often addresses the environmental issue in much of her research, she also looks at the biological issue in her book *The Argument Culture*. Tannen states, "Surely a biological component plays a part in the greater use of antagonism among men, but cultural influence can override biological inheritance" (Tannen, *Argument* 205). She sums up the nature versus nurture issue by saying, "the patterns that typify women's and men's styles of opposition and conflict are the result of both biology and culture" (207).

Lillian Glass addresses the issue that different hormones found in men and women's bodies make them act differently and therefore communicate differently. She also discusses how brain development has been found to relate to sex differences.

Judy Mann says, "Most experts now believe that what happens to boys and girls is a complex interaction between slight biological differences and tremendously powerful social forces that begin to manifest themselves the minute the parents find out whether they are going to have a boy or a girl" (qtd. in McCluskey 6).

The writer now uses the sources to explain the consequences of communication failures on both men and women.

Consequences of Gender Differences

Now that we have looked at different styles of gender communication and possible causes of gender

Holz 5

communication, let us look at the possible results. Morgan and Coleman relate that divorce is one of the most stressful events a person can experience. They expound upon this point by stating, "The decision to divorce is typically made with ambivalence, uncertainty and confusion. It is a difficult step. The family identity changes, and the identities of the individuals involved change as well."

Through various studies, Tannen has concluded that men and women have different purposes for engaging in communication. She explains the different ways men and women handle communication throughout the day. She explains that a man constantly talks during his workday in order to impress those around him and to establish his status in the office. At home he wants peace and quiet. On the other hand, a woman is constantly cautious and guarded about what she says during her workday. Women try hard to avoid confrontation and avoid offending anyone with their language. So when a woman comes home from work she expects to be able to talk freely without having to guard her words. The consequence? The woman expects conversation, but the man is tired of talking (Tannen, *He Said*).

Solutions

Answers for better gender communication seem elusive. What can be done about this apparent gap in communication between genders? In his article published on *Forbes.com*, Charles Salzberg offers the obvious suggestion that women should make an attempt to understand the male model of communication and that men should make an attempt to understand the female model of communication.

The writer now depends on the sources to provide possible solutions.

However, in his article "Speaking Across the Gender Gap," David Cohen mentions that experts didn't think it

Holz 6

would be helpful to teach men to communicate more like women and women to communicate more like men. This attempt would prove unproductive because it would go against what men and women have been taught since birth. Rather than change the genders to be more like one another, we could simply try to "understand" each other better.

In addition, Carolyn Crozier makes this observation, "The idea that women should translate their experiences into the male code in order to express themselves effectively . . . is an outmoded, inconsistent, subservient notion that should no longer be given credibility in modern society." She suggests three things we can change; (1) Change the norm by which leadership success is judged; (2) Redefine what we mean by power; and (3) Become more sensitive to the places and times when inequity and inequality occur (Crozier). Similarly, Patel offers advice to help combat "cross-cultural" fights. He suggests (1) Identify your fighting style; (2) Agree on rules of engagement; and (3) Identify the real issue behind the conflict (Patel).

McCluskey claims men and women need honest communication that shows respect, and they must "manage conflict in a way that maintains the relationship and gets the job done" (5). She says, "To improve relationships and interactions between men and women, we must acknowledge the differences that do exist, understand how they develop, and discard dogma about what are the 'right' roles of women and men" (5).

Obviously, differences exist in the way men and women communicate, whether caused by biological and/or environmental factors. We can consider the possible causes, the consequences, and possible solutions. Using this knowledge, we should be able to more accurately interpret communication between the genders.

Holz 7

Works Cited

The separate Works Cited page gives full information on each source cited in the paper.

Basow, Susan A., and Kimberly Rubenfeld. "'Troubles Talk':
    Effects of Gender and Gender Typing." *Sex Roles: A*
    Journal of Research 48. (2003): 183–187. *Expanded*
    Academic. Web. 19 Apr. 2012.

Cohen, David. "Speaking Across the Gender Gap." *New*
    Scientist 131.1783 (1991): 36. *Expanded Academic*.
    Web. 20 Apr. 2012.

Crozier, Carolyn Y. "Subservient Speech: Women Need to be
    Heard." 8 Aug. 2010. Web. 15 Apr. 2012.

Glass, Lillian. *He Says, She Says: Closing the Communication*
    Gap Between the Sexes. New York: Putnam, 1993. Print.

James, Tammy, and Bethann Cinelli. "Exploring Gender-
    Based Communication Styles." *Journal of School Health*
    73 (2003): 41–42. *Access My Library*. Web. 17 Apr.
    2012.

McCluskey, Karen Curnow. "Gender at Work." *Public*
    Management 79.5 (1997): 5–10. *Questia*. Web. 18 Apr.
    2012.

Morgan, Marni, and Marilyn Coleman. "Focus on Families:
    Divorce and Adults." Apr. 2007. Web. 17 Apr. 2012.

Patel, Kawa. "Do Men and Women Speak the Same
    Language?" 14 Nov. 2010. Web. 18 Apr. 2012.

Salzberg, Carl. "He Said, She Heard." *Forbes.com*. 24 Nov.
    2009. Web. 19 Apr. 2012.

Tannen, Deborah. *The Argument Culture: Moving from*
    Debate to Dialogue. New York: Random House, 2004.
    Print.

---. *He Said, She Said: Exploring the Different Ways Men and*
    Women Communicate. CD. New York: Barnes & Noble,
    2004. Print.

---. *You Just Don't Understand: Women and Men in*
    Conversation. New York: HarperCollins, 2007. Print.

Holz 8

Witt, Susan D. "Parental Influence on Children's
    Socialization to Gender Roles." *Adolescence* 32 (1997):
    253. *Access My Library*. Web. 17 Apr. 2012.
Woods, Julia T. *Gendered Lives*. 9th ed. San Francisco:
    Wadsworth, 2010. Print.

9

Drafting the Paper in an Academic Style

Clear Targets

Your research project should examine a subject in depth, and also examine *your* knowledge and the strength of *your* evidence. This chapter will help you find the style necessary for your field of study and will show you how to:

- Focus your argument for your field of study
- Draft and revise the research paper
- Create an introduction, a body, and a conclusion

As you draft your paper, your voice should flow from one idea to the next smoothly and logically. Moreover, you should adopt an academic style that presents a fair, balanced treatment of the subject. Mentioning opposing viewpoints early in a report gives you something to work against and may strengthen your conclusion. Keep in mind negative findings because they have value and should be reported even if they contradict your original hypothesis (see pages 113–115 for more on the logic and ethics of a presentation).

Three principles for drafting may serve your needs:

- *Be practical.* Write portions of the paper when you are ready, skipping over sections of your outline. Leave plenty of space for notes and corrections.
- *Be uninhibited.* Write without fear or delay because initial drafts are attempts to get words on the page rather than to create a polished document.
- *Be conscientious about citations.* Cite the names of the sources in your notes and text, enclose quotations, and preserve page numbers to the sources.

9a Writing for Your Field of Study

Each discipline has its own special language, style of expression, and manuscript format. In time, you will learn fully the style for your college major, for there are distinctions in the writing styles for papers in the humanities, the social sciences, and the physical sciences.

Academic Style in the Humanities

Writing in one of the humanities will require you to adopt a certain style, as shown in the following example:

> Organ and tissue donation is the gift of life. Each year many people confront health problems due to diseases or congenital birth defects. Tom Taddonia explains that tissues such as skin, veins, and valves can be used to correct congenital defects, blindness, visual impairment, trauma, burns, dental defects, arthritis, cancer, vascular and heart disease (34). Steve Barnill says, "More than 400 people each month receive the gift of sight through yet another type of tissue donation—corneal transplants. In many cases, donors unsuitable for organ donation are eligible for tissue donation." Barnill notes that tissues are now used in orthopedic surgery, cardiovascular surgery, plastic surgery, dentistry, and podiatry. Even so, not enough people are willing to donate organs and tissues.

Writing in the humanities is often concerned with the quality of life, of art, and of ideas, and has the following traits:

- Use of the present tense to indicate that this problem is an enduring one for humans of past ages as well as the present and the future
- Use of MLA style
- Discussion of theory as supported by the literature

Academic Style in the Social Sciences

A social science student, using APA style, might write the same passage as shown:

> Organ and tissue donation has been identified as a social as well as medical problem in the United States. On one side, people have confronted serious problems in securing organs

and tissue to correct health problems; on the other, people have demonstrated a reluctance to donate their organs. This need has been identified by Taddonia (2012), Barnill (2011), Ruskin (2009), and others. This hypothesis remains: People are reluctant to sign the donor cards. Consequently, this study will survey a random set of 1,000 persons who have drivers' licenses. The tabulations will indicate reasons for signing or not signing for donation. Further investigation can then be conducted to determine ways of increasing participation by potential donors.

With an objective approach to the topic, writing in the social sciences displays these characteristics:

- A scientific plan for examining a hypothesis
- Preference for the passive voice
- Minimal quotations from the sources, anticipating that readers will examine the literature for themselves
- An indication of the study's purpose and/or a general plan for empirical research
- Use of APA style for documenting the sources
- Use of past tense or the present perfect tense in references to the source material
- Awareness that this research will prompt further study

Academic Style in the Physical and Medical Sciences

A medical student might write on this same topic, as shown in CSE number style:

Taddonia (1) has shown that human tissue can be used to correct many defects. Barnill (2) showed that more than 400 people receive corneal transplants each month. Yet the health profession needs more donors. It has been shown (3–6) that advanced care directives by patients with terminal illnesses would improve the donation of organs and tissue and relieve relatives of making any decision. Patients have been encouraged to complete organ donation cards (7) as well as to sign living wills (5, 8), special powers of attorney (5), and DNR (Do Not Resuscitate) Orders (5, 8). It is encouraged that advanced care directives become standard for the terminally ill.

Scientific writing, like the passage above, typically features some of these traits:

- An objective approach to the topic without signs of personal commitment
- A search for a professional position (i.e., on organ donation)
- A preference for the passive voice and for past tense verbs
- A preference for the CSE citation-sequence system or, in some cases, the name-year system (see the example above)
- A reluctance to quote from the sources

9b Focusing Your Argument

Your writing style in the research paper needs to be factual, but it should also reflect your ideas on the topic. You will be able to draft your paper more quickly if you focus on the key issue(s). Each paragraph should build on and amplify your primary claim.

Persuading, Inquiring, and Negotiating

Establishing a purpose for writing is one way to focus your argument. Do you wish to persuade, inquire, or negotiate? Most research papers make an inquiry.

Persuasion means that you wish to convince the reader that your position is valid and, perhaps, to take action. For example:

> Research has shown that homeowners and wild animals cannot live together in harmony. Thus, we need to establish green zones in every city of this country to control the sprawl in urban areas and to protect a segment of the natural habitat for the animals.

Inquiry is an exploratory approach to a problem in which you examine the issues without the insistence of persuasion. It is a truth-seeking adventure. You will often need to examine, test, or observe in order to discuss the implications of the research. For example:

> Many suburban homedwellers complain that deer, raccoons, and other wild animals ravage their gardens, flowerbeds, and garbage cans; however, the animals were there first. Thus, we need a task force to examine the rights of each side in this conflict.

Negotiation is a search for a solution. It means that you attempt to resolve a conflict by inventing options or a mediated solution. For example:

> Suburban neighbors need to find ways to embrace the wild animals that have been displaced rather than voice anger at the animals or the county government. Research has shown that green zones and wilderness trails would solve some of the problems; however, such a solution would require serious negotiations with real estate developers who want to use every square foot of every development.

Maintaining a Focus with Ethical and Logical Appeals

As an objective writer, you will need to examine the problem, make your claim, and provide supporting evidence. Moderation of your voice, even during argument, suggests control of the situation, both emotionally and intellectually. Your voice alerts the audience to your point of view in two ways:

- **Ethical appeal.** If you project the image of one who knows and cares about the topic, the reader will recognize and respect your deep interest in the subject and the way you have carefully crafted your argument. The reader will also appreciate your attention to research conventions.
- **Logical appeal.** For readers to believe in your position, you must provide sufficient evidence in the form of statistical data, paraphrases, and direct quotations from authorities on the subject.

The issue of organ donation, for example, elicits different reactions. Some people argue from the logical position that organs are available and should be used for those in need. Others argue from the ethical position that organs might be harvested prematurely or that organ donation violates religious principles. As a writer, you must balance your ethical and logical appeals to your readers.

Focusing the Final Thesis or Hypothesis

Refining your thesis may keep your paper on track. A thesis expresses a theory that you hope to support with evidence and arguments. A hypothesis is a theory that you hope to prove by investigating, testing, and/or observing. Both the thesis and the hypothesis are propositions that you want to maintain, analyze, and prove. A final thesis or hypothesis performs three tasks:

1. Establishes a claim to control and focuses the entire paper
2. Provides unity and a sense of direction
3. Specifies to the reader the point of the research

For example, one student started with the topic "exorbitant tuition," narrowed it to the phrase "tuition fees put parents in debt," and ultimately crafted this thesis:

> The exorbitant tuition at America's colleges is forcing out the poor and promoting an elitist class.

The statement above focuses the argument on the effects of high fees on enrollment. The student needs to prove the assertion by gathering and tabulating statistics.

Questions Will Focus the Thesis

If you have trouble finding a claim or argument, ask yourself a few questions. One of the answers might serve as the thesis or the hypothesis.

- What is the point of my research?

HYPOTHESIS: A delicate balance of medicine, diet, and exercise can control diabetes mellitus.

- Can I tell the reader anything new or different?

HYPOTHESIS: Most well water in Rutherford County is unsafe for drinking.

- Do I have a solution to the problem?

THESIS: Public support for "safe" houses will provide a haven for children who are abused by their parents.

- Do I have a new slant and new approach to the issue?

HYPOTHESIS: Poverty, not greed, forces many youngsters into a life of crime.

- Should I take the minority view of this matter?

THESIS: Give credit where it is due: Custer may have lost the battle at Little Bighorn, but Crazy Horse and his men, with inspiration from Sitting Bull, won the battle.

- Will an enthymeme serve my purpose by making a claim in a *because* clause?

ENTHYMEME: Sufficient organ and tissue donation, enough to satisfy the demand, remains almost impossible because negative myths and religious concerns dominate the minds of many people.

Key Words Will Focus the Thesis or the Hypothesis

Use the important words from your notes and rough outline to refine your thesis sentence. For example, during your reading of several novels or short stories by Flannery O'Connor, you might have jotted down certain repetitions of image, theme, or character. The key words might be *death*, *ironic moments of humor*, *hysteria and passion*, *human shortcomings*, or other issues that O'Connor repeatedly explored. These concrete ideas might point you toward a general thesis:

> The tragic endings of Flannery O'Connor's stories depict desperate people coming face to face with their own shortcomings.

Change Your Thesis but Not Your Hypothesis

Be willing to abandon your preliminary thesis if research leads you to new and different issues. However, a hypothesis *cannot* be adjusted or changed. It will be proved true, partially true, or untrue. Your negative findings have value, for you will have disproved the hypothesis so that others need not duplicate your research. For example, the hypothesis might assert: "Industrial pollution is seeping into water tables and traveling many miles into neighboring well water of Lamar County." Your report may prove the truth of the hypothesis, but it may not. It may only establish a probability and the need for additional research.

CHECKLIST

Writing the Final Thesis or Hypothesis

You should be able to answer "yes" to each question below:

- Does the thesis express your position in a full, declarative statement that is not a question, not a statement of purpose, and not merely a topic?
- Does it limit the subject to a narrow focus that grows out of research?
- Does it establish an investigation, interpretation, or theoretical presentation?
- Does it point forward to your findings and a discussion of the implications in your conclusion?

9c Writing an Academic Title

A clearly expressed title, like a good thesis statement, focuses your writing and keeps you on course. Although writing a final title may not be feasible until the paper is written, the preliminary title can provide specific words of identification to help you stay focused. For example, one writer began with the title: "Diabetes." Then, to make it more specific, the writer added another word to make "Diabetes Management." As research developed and she recognized the role of medicine, diet, and exercise for victims, she refined the title even more: "Diabetes Management: A Delicate Balance of Medicine, Diet, and Exercise." Thereby, she and her readers had a clear idea that the paper was about three methods of managing the disease.

Long titles are standard in scholarly writing. Consider the following examples:

1. Subject, colon, and focusing phrase:

   Organ and Tissue Donation and Transplantation: Myths, Ethical Issues, and Lives Saved

2. Subject, focusing prepositional phrase:

   Gothic Madness in Three Southern Writers

3. Subject, colon, and type of study:

   Black Dialect in Maya Angelou's Poetry: A Language Study

4. Subject, colon, and focusing question:

   AIDS: Where Did It Come From?

5. Subject, comparative study:

   Religious Imagery in N. Scott Momaday's *The Names* and Heronimous Storm's *Seven Arrows*

For placement of the title, see one of these examples: MLA, pages 101 and 150; APA, page 167; CMS, page 184; and CSE, page 194.

9d Drafting the Paper

As you begin drafting your research report, work systematically through your research journal, preliminary plan, or outline to keep order as your notes expand your research (see pages 78–89 for models of organization). Use your notes, photocopies, downloaded material, and research journal to transfer materials directly into the text, remembering always to provide citations to borrowed information. Do not quote an entire paragraph unless it is crucial to your discussion and you cannot easily reduce it to a summary. In addition, be conscious of basic writing conventions, as described next.

Writing with Unity and Coherence

Unity refers to exploring one topic in depth to give your writing a single vision. With unity, each paragraph carefully expands upon a single aspect of the narrowed subject. **Coherence** connects the parts logically by:

- Repetition of key words and sentence structures
- The judicious use of pronouns and synonyms
- The effective placement of transitional words and phrases (e.g., *also, furthermore, therefore, in addition*, and *thus*)

The next passage reads with unity (it keeps its focus) and coherence (it repeats key words and uses transitions effectively, as shown in highlighted type).

> Talk shows are spectacles and forms of dramatic entertainment; therefore, members of the studio audience are acting out parts in the drama, like a Greek chorus, just as the host, the guest, and the television viewers are actors as well. Furthermore, some sort of interaction with the "characters" in this made-for-television "drama" happens all the time. If we read a book or attend a play, we question the text, we question the presentation, and we determine for ourselves what it means to us.

Writing in the Proper Tense

Verb tense often distinguishes a paper in the humanities from one in the natural and social sciences. Use the **past tense** in the social sciences and the physical sciences (see pages 110–112) . Use the **present tense** in the humanities. MLA style employs the present tense to cite an author's work (e.g., "Patel *explains*" or "the work of Scoggin and Rodriguez *shows*"). The ideas and the words of the writers remain in print and continue to be true in the universal present. Therefore, when writing a paper in the humanities, use the historical present tense, as shown here:

> "It was the best of times, it was the worst of times," writes Charles Dickens about the eighteenth century.

```
Johnson [argues] that sociologist Norman Wayman has
a "narrow-minded view of clerics and their role in the
community" (64).
```

Using the Language of the Discipline

Every discipline and every topic has its own vocabulary. Therefore, while reading and taking notes, jot down words and phrases relevant to your research study. Get comfortable with them so you can use them effectively. For example, a child abuse topic requires the language of sociology and psychology, thereby demanding an acquaintance with the following terms:

social worker	maltreatment	aggressive behavior
poverty levels	guardians	hostility
stress	battered child	incestuous relations
formative years	recurrence	behavioral patterns

Many writers create a terminology list to strengthen their command of appropriate nouns and verbs for the subject in question.

Using Source Material to Enhance Your Writing

Readers want to see your thoughts and ideas on a subject. For this reason, a paragraph should seldom contain source material only; it must contain a topic sentence to establish a point for the research evidence. Every paragraph should explain, analyze, and support a thesis, not merely string together a set of quotations. The following passage effectively cites two different sources.

```
Two factors that have played a part in farmland becoming
drought prone are "[light, sandy soil and soils with high]
[alkalinity]" (Boughman 234). In response, [Bjornson says]
[that drought resistant plants exist along parts of the]
[Mediterranean Sea]. Thus, hybrids of these plants may serve
Texas farmers [(34).]
```

The short passage weaves the sources effectively into a whole, uses the sources as a natural extension of the discussion, and cites each source separately with appropriate citations.

Writing in the Third Person

Write your paper with third-person narration, avoiding phrasing such as "I believe" or "It is my opinion." Rather than writing, "I think television violence affects children," drop the opening two words and write,

"Television violence affects children." Readers will understand that the statement is your thought and one that you will defend with evidence.

Writing with the Passive Voice in an Appropriate Manner

The passive voice is often less forceful than an active verb. However, research writers sometimes need to use the passive voice verb, as shown here:

> Forty-three students of a third-grade class at Barksdale Elementary School were observed for two weeks.

Use of the passive voice is fairly standard in the social sciences and the natural or applied sciences. The passive voice is preferred because it keeps the focus on the subject of the research, not the writer (you would not want to say, "I observed the students").

Placing Graphics Effectively in a Research Essay

Use graphics to support your text. Most computers allow you to create tables, line graphs, or pie charts as well as diagrams, maps, and other original designs. You may also import tables and illustrations from your sources. Place these graphics as close as possible to the parts of the text to which they relate. It is acceptable to use full-color art if your printer will print in colors; however, use black for the captions and date. Place a full-page graphic design on a separate sheet after making a textual reference to it (e.g., "see Table 7"). Place graphic designs in an appendix when you have several complex items that might distract the reader from your textual message. See page 209 in the Appendix for help with designing tables, line graphs, illustrations, pie charts, and other visuals.

Avoiding Sexist and Biased Language

The best writers exercise caution against words that may stereotype any person, regardless of gender, race, nationality, creed, age, sexual orientation, or disability. The following are some guidelines to help you avoid discriminatory language.

Age

Review the accuracy of your statement of age. It is appropriate to use *boy* and *girl* for children of high school age and under. *Young man* and *young woman* or *male adolescent* and *female adolescent* can be appropriate, but *teenager* carries a certain bias. Avoid *elderly* as a noun; use *older persons*.

Gender

Gender is a matter of our culture that identifies men and women within their social groups. *Sex* tends to be a biological factor (see below for a discussion of sexual orientation).

- Use plural subjects so that nonspecific, plural pronouns are grammatically correct. For example, you may specify that Judy Jones maintains *her* lab equipment in sterile condition or indicate that technicians, in general, maintain *their* own equipment.
- Reword the sentence so that a pronoun is unnecessary, as in *The doctor prepared the necessary surgical equipment without interference.*
- Use pronouns that denote gender only when necessary and only when gender has been previously established, as in *Mary, as a new laboratory technician, must learn to maintain her equipment in sterile condition.*
- Use *woman* or *women* in most instances (e.g., *a woman's intuition*), except use *female* for species and statistics (e.g., *four female subjects*). Avoid the use of *lady*, as in *lady pilot*.
- Use a person's full name (e.g., Ernest Hemingway or Joan Didion) when first mentioned; thereafter use only the surname (e.g., Hemingway or Didion). In general, avoid formal titles (e.g., Dr., Gen., Mrs., Ms., Lt., or Professor) and their equivalents in other languages (e.g., Mme., Dame, or Monsieur).
- Avoid unparallel terms such as *man and wife* or *7 men and 16 females*. Keep terms parallel by saying *husband and wife* or *man and woman* and *7 male rats and 16 female rats*.

Sexual Orientation

The term *sexual orientation* is preferred to the term *sexual preference*. It is preferable to use *lesbians* and *gay men* rather than *homosexuals*. The terms *heterosexual, homosexual,* and *bisexual* can be used to describe both the identity and the behavior of subjects.

Ethnic and Racial Identity

Some persons prefer the term *Black*, others prefer *African American*, and still others prefer *a person of color*. The terms *Negro* and *Afro-American* are dated and inappropriate. Use *Black* and *White*, not the lowercase *black* and *white*. In like manner, some individuals may prefer *Hispanic or Latino*. Use the term *Asian* or *Asian American* rather than *Oriental*. *Native American* is a broad term that includes *Samoans, Hawaiians,* and *American Indians*. A good rule of thumb is to use a person's nationality when it is known (*Mexican, Canadian, Comanche,* or *Nigerian*).

Disability

In general, place people first, not their disability. Rather than *disabled person* or *retarded child* say *person who has scoliosis* or *a child with Down syndrome*. Avoid saying *a challenged person* or *a special child* in favor of *a person with* or *a child with*. Remember that a *disability* is a physical quality, while a *handicap* is a limitation that might be imposed by nonphysical factors, such as stairs or poverty or social attitudes.

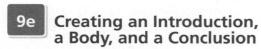

9e Creating an Introduction, a Body, and a Conclusion

Writing the Introduction

Use the first few paragraphs of your paper to establish the nature of your study.

SUBJECT:	Does your introduction identify your specific topic, and then define, limit, and narrow it to one issue?
BACKGROUND:	Does your introduction provide relevant historical data or discuss a few key sources that touch on your specific issue?
PROBLEM:	Does your introduction identify a problem and explain the complications that your research paper will explore or resolve?
THESIS:	Does your introduction use your thesis or hypothesis within the first few paragraphs to establish the direction of the study and to point your readers toward your eventual conclusions?

How you work these essential elements into the beginning of your paper will depend upon your style of writing. They need not appear in this order. Nor should you cram all these items into a short opening paragraph. Feel free to write a long introduction by using more than one of these techniques:

- Open with your thesis or hypothesis.
- Open with a quotation.
- Relate your topic to the well known.
- Provide background information.
- Review the literature.

- Provide a brief summary.
- Define key terms.
- Supply data, statistics, and special evidence.
- Take exception to critical views.
- Use an anecdote as a hook to draw your reader into the essay.

The following sample of an introduction gives background information, establishes a persuasive position, reviews key literature, takes exception, gives key terms, and offers a thesis.

John Berendt's popular and successful novel *Midnight in the Garden of Good and Evil* skillfully presents the unpredictable twists and turns of a landmark murder case set under the moss-hung live oaks of Savannah, Georgia. While it is written as a novel, the nonfiction account of this tragic murder case reveals the intriguing and sometimes deranged relationships that thrive in a town where everyone knows everyone else. However, the mystique of the novel does not lie with the murder case but with the collection of unusual and often complex characters, including a voodoo priestess, a young Southern gigolo, and a black drag queen (e.g., Bilkin, Miller, and especially Carson, who describes the people of Savannah as "a type of Greek chorus" [14]). Berendt's success lies in his carefully crafted characterization.

Writing the Body of the Research Paper

When writing the body, you should keep in mind three elements:

ANALYSIS: Classify the major issues of the study and provide a careful analysis of each in defense of your thesis.

PRESENTATION: Provide well-reasoned statements at the beginning of your paragraphs and supply evidence of support with proper documentation.

PARAGRAPHS: Offer a variety of development to compare, show process, narrate the history of the subject, and show causes.

Use these techniques to build substantive paragraphs for your paper:

- Relate a time sequence.
- Compare or contrast issues, the views of experts, and the nature of literary characters.

- Develop cause and effect.
- Issue a call to action.
- Define key terminology.
- Show a process.
- Ask questions and provide answers.
- Cite evidence from source materials.
- Explain the methods used and the design of the study.
- Present the results of the investigation with data, statistics, and graphics.

The following paragraph demonstrates the use of several techniques—an overview of the problem, citing a source, comparing issues, cause and effect, key terms, and process.

> To burn or not to burn the natural forests in the national parks is the question. The pyrophobia public voices its protests while environmentalists praise the rejuvenating effects of a good forest fire. It is difficult to convince people that not all fire is bad. The public has visions of Smokey the Bear campaigns and mental images of Bambi and Thumper fleeing the roaring flames. Chris Bolgiano explains that federal policy evolved slowly "from the basic impulse to douse all fires immediately to a sophisticated decision matrix based on the functions of any given unit of land" (23). Bolgiano declares that "timber production, grazing, recreation, and wilderness preservation elicit different fire-management approaches" (23).

Writing the Conclusion of the Paper

The conclusion is not a summary; it is a discussion of beliefs and findings based on your reasoning and on the evidence and results you have presented. Select appropriate items from this list.

THESIS: Reaffirm the thesis, the hypothesis, or the central mission of your study. If appropriate, give a statement in support or nonsupport of an original enthymeme or hypothesis.

JUDGMENT: Discuss and interpret the findings. Give answers. Now is the time to draw inferences, to emphasize a theory, and to find relevance in the results.

DIRECTIVES: Based on the theoretical implications of the study, offer suggestions for action and for new research.

DISCUSSION: Discuss the implications of your findings from testing or observation.

Use these techniques to write the conclusion:

- Restate the thesis and reach beyond it.
- Close with an effective quotation.
- Return the focus of a literary study to the author.
- Compare the past to the present.
- Offer a directive or a solution.
- Give a call to action.
- Discuss the implications of your findings.

The following example of a conclusion provides an interpretation of the results of an experiment as well as the implications of the results.

> The results of this experiment were similar to expectations, but perhaps the statistical significance, because of the small subject size, was biased toward the delayed conditions of the curve. Barker and Peay have addressed this point. The subjects were not truly representative of the total population because of their prior exposure to test procedures. Another factor that may have affected the curves was the presentation of the data. The images on the screen were available for five seconds, and that amount of time may have enabled the subjects to store each image effectively. If the time period for each image were reduced to one or two seconds, there could be lower recall scores, thereby reducing the differences between the control group and the experimental group.

9f Revising the Rough Draft

Once you have the complete paper in a rough draft, the serious business of editing begins. First, you should revise your paper on a global scale, moving blocks of material around so that information is presented logically and in the correct style. Second, edit the draft with a line-by-line examination of wording and technical excellence. Third, proofread the final version to assure that your words are spelled correctly and the text is grammatically sound.

Revision can turn a passable paper into an excellent one. Revise the manuscript on a global scale by looking at its overall design. Do the introduction, body, and conclusion have substance? Do the paragraphs maintain the flow of your central proposition? Does the paper fulfill the requirements of the academic model?

Editing before Printing the Final Manuscript

Global revision is complemented by careful editing of paragraphs, sentences, and individual words. Travel through the paper to study your citation of the sources. Confirm that you have properly cited each quoted or paraphrased source. Use your spell-checker and then re-read your paper, looking for misspellings. Here are eight additional tasks:

1. Cut phrases and sentences that do not advance your main ideas or that merely repeat what your sources have already stated.
2. Determine that coordinated, balanced ideas are appropriately expressed and that minor ideas are properly subordinated.
3. Change most of your "to be" verbs (is, are, was) to stronger active verbs.
4. Maintain the present tense of most verbs.
5. Convert passive structures to active unless you want to emphasize the subject, not the actor (see pages 117–119).
6. Confirm that you have introduced paraphrases and quotations so that they flow smoothly in your text.
7. Use formal, academic style and be on guard against clusters of little monosyllabic words that fail to advance ideas. Examine your wording for its effectiveness within the context of your subject (see pages 110–112).
8. Examine your paragraphs for effective transitions that move the reader from one paragraph to the next.

Using the Computer to Edit Your Text

Some software programs will examine your grammar and mechanics, look for parentheses that you opened but never closed, find unpaired quotation marks, flag passive verbs, question your spelling, and mark other items for your correction. Pay attention to the caution flags raised by this type of program. After a software program examines the style of your manuscript, you should revise and edit the text to improve stylistic weaknesses. Remember, it is your paper, not the computer's document, so use your knowledge of grammar and writing mechanics when making revisions.

Participating in Peer Review

Peer review has two sides. First, it means handing your paper to a friend or classmate, asking for their opinions and suggestions. Second, it means reviewing a classmate's research paper. You can learn by reviewing as well as by writing. Your instructor may supply a peer review sheet, or you can use the accompanying checklist. Criticize the paper constructively on each point.

CHECKLIST

Peer Review

1. Are the subject and the accompanying issues introduced early?

2. Is the writer's critical approach to the problem stated clearly in a thesis sentence? Is it placed effectively in the introduction?

3. Do the paragraphs of the body have individual unity? That is, does each one develop an important idea and only one idea? Does each paragraph relate to the thesis?

4. Are sources introduced, usually with the name of the expert, and then cited by a page number within parentheses? Keep in mind that Internet sources will not have page numbers.

5. Is it clear where a paraphrase begins and where it ends?

6. Are the sources relevant to the argument?

7. Does the writer weave quotations into the text effectively while avoiding long quotations that look like filler instead of substance?

8. Does the conclusion arrive at a resolution about the central issue?

9. Does the title describe clearly what your classmate has put in the body of the paper?

Proofreading

Print a hard copy of your manuscript. Proofread this final version with great care before submitting it to your instructor.

CHECKLIST

Proofreading

1. Check for errors in sentence structure, spelling, and punctuation.

2. Check for hyphenation and word division. Remember that no words should be hyphenated at the ends of lines.

3. Read each quotation to ensure that your own wording and the words within your quoted materials are accurate. Check for opening and closing quotation marks.

4. Double-check in-text citations to be certain that each one is correct and that each source is listed on your Works Cited page at the end of the paper.

5. Double-check the format—the title page, margins, spacing, content notes, and other elements.

10

Using MLA Style

Clear Targets

Devoted to the documentation style of the Modern Language Association (MLA), this chapter provides guidelines and standards for research writing in English studies, literature, English usage, and the foreign languages. The following components discussed in this chapter will help to unify and accurately document your research paper:

- Blending sources into your writing
- Punctuating citations properly and consistently
- Writing Works Cited references in MLA style
- Formatting the paper in MLA style

The MLA documentation style gives all scholars in the field a consistent way to consult the sources that are cited in your project.

10a Blending Sources into Your Writing

The MLA style requires the full names of a source's author(s) on first mention and the last name(s) thereafter.

Ralph Templeton examines in depth the animal imagery in Thomas Hardy's novels (53–54).

However, mention the last name(s) only in parenthetical citations, even the first.

One source has examined in depth the animal imagery in Thomas Hardy's novels (Templeton 53–54).

Quotations, paraphrases, and summaries should support your topic sentences, and they contribute coherence if they extend a paragraph's argument. A collection of random quotations is unacceptable. Notice how the following example introduces the idea of executive power and develops it with citations.

> The power of the executive mansion began in November 1801 when John Adams, accompanied by a single secretary and servant, entered "the unfinished White House that smelled of plaster and paint" (Olson 23). One of his first tasks was to write a letter to his wife Abigail. According to Richard Striker, voters must always consider the words that Adams used on that first day in the White House: "May none but honest and wise men ever rule under this roof" (qtd. in Striker 78). At no other time are these simple words more compelling than when the nation considers candidates for the highest office during an election.

Note: Keep in-text citations brief. Remember, your readers will have full documentation to each source on the Works Cited page (see Section 10c, pages 136–148).

Identifying the Author and Page Number

Sometimes you will need no parenthetical citation if the names are provided from an Internet site.

> The women of Thomas Hardy's novels are the special focus of three essays by Nancy Norris, Judith Mitchell, and James Scott.

Introduce a quotation or a paraphrase with the author's name and close it with a page number, placed inside the parentheses.

> Herbert Norfleet states that the use of video games by children improves their hand and eye coordination (45).

You may also place a last name with the page number at the end of a quotation or paraphrase.

> "Strung along the Georgia coast are fascinating ruins of forts and commercial buildings from the 18th century, all constructed with a form of cement reinforced with seashells" (Roberts 245).

HINT: In MLA style, do not place a comma between the name and the page number.

Sometimes notes at the end of a quotation make it expeditious to place the page number immediately after the name.

> Rizarrio (34) urges businesses to "stop the ridiculous practice of <u>overlighting</u> with brighter signs and entrance lights" (emphasis added).

Citing a Source When No Author Is Listed

When no author is shown on a title page, cite the title of the article, the name of the magazine, the name of a bulletin or book, or the name of the publishing organization.

> The mutual fund market has shown a significant increase in activity during the past ten years and has yet to reach its peak (*Annual Report 2012* 12).

HINT: Shorten titles to a key word for the citation, such as *Annual Report*, rather than the full title, *2011 Annual Report of the St. Petersburg Arts Council.*

Citing Nonprint Sources That Have No Page Numbers

You may need to identify a speech, song lyric, interview, or television program. Because no page numbers for it exist, omit the parenthetical citation and, instead, mention the type of source so that readers will not expect page numbers.

> Salcedo's lecture emphasized that too many individuals "consider themselves invulnerable and much too crafty to be caught shoplifting—until they are actually caught."

Citing Internet Sources

Internet sources typically have no prescribed page numbers or numbered paragraphs.

> Hershel Winthrop interprets Hawthorne's stories as the search for holiness in a corrupt Puritan society.

If you cannot identify an author, give the article title or website information.

One website claims that any diet that avoids carbohydrates
will avoid some sugars that are essential for the body
("Fad Diets").

Citing Indirect Sources

Sometimes the writer of a book or article will quote another person from an interview or personal correspondence. If you want to
use such a quotation, conform to this next example, which cites the
person making the statement (Greenburg) and then cites the source
where the material was found (Peterson).

After students get beyond middle school, they begin to resent
interference by their parents, especially in school activities.
They need some space from Mom and Dad. Martin Greenburg
says, "The interventions can be construed by the adolescent as
negative, overburdening and interfering with the child's ability
to care for himself" (qtd. in Peterson 9A).

Without the reference to Greenburg, it would be difficult to find the
article in the Works Cited list; moreover, readers would assume that
Peterson had spoken the words.

Citing Material from Textbooks and Large Anthologies

If you quote from a textbook or anthology, cite only the author and
the page of the text. The Works Cited entry will provide full details
(see Section 10c, pages 136–148).

In "How to Tell a True War Story," Tim O'Brien reminds readers
that "war is hell, but that's not the half of it, because war
is also mystery and terror and adventure and courage and
discovery and holiness and pity and despair and longing and
love" (465).

Adding Information to In-Text Citations

A detailed citation, such as "(*Great Expectations* 681; chap. 4)," will
enable the reader to locate the passage. The next citation shows several authors listed within one citation:

Several sources have suggested that Nashville, Tennessee, the
Music City, borders between reality and fantasy as the last

place where the American dream of country singers can become reality (Bales 98–99; Riggins 55; Earley 261–63).

10b Punctuating Citations Properly and Consistently

Keep parenthetical citations outside quotation marks but inside the final period, as shown here:

Yaffe says what we talk about when we talk about jazz is "the provenance of metaphor: Ellison's *Invisible Man* looking toward Louis Armstrong as his muse" (123).

HINT: Do not use *p.* or *pp.* with the page number(s) when using the MLA style.

The example below shows how to place commas.

"Modern advertising," says Rachel Murphy, "not only creates a marketplace, it determines values." She adds, "I resist the advertiser's argument that they 'awaken, not create' desires'" (192).

Both semicolons and colons go outside the quotation marks.

Brian Sutton-Smith says, "Adults don't worry whether <u>their</u> toys are educational" (64); nevertheless, parents want to keep their children in a learning mode.

When a question mark or an exclamation mark is a part of the quotation, keep it inside the quotation mark.

Thompson (16) passionately shouted to union members, "We can bring order into our lives even though we face hostility from every quarter!"

Retain question marks and exclamation marks when the quotation begins a sentence.

"We face hostility from every quarter!" declared the union leader.

Place question marks inside the closing quotation mark when they are part of the original quotation; otherwise, they go outside.

The philosopher Brackenridge (16) asks, "How should we order our lives?"

but

> Did Brackenridge (16) say that we might encounter "hostility from every quarter"?

Single quotation marks signal a quotation within a quotation.

> Newspaper columnist George Will speaks of baseball's Hall of Fame as "a shrine to baseball's 'immortals'" (94).

Indenting Long Quotations

Set off long prose quotations of four lines or more by indenting one inch, two clicks of the tab key, or ten spaces. Do not use quotation marks with the indented material. Place the parenthetical citation *after* the final mark of punctuation, as shown below:

> According to the National Heritage Network, humans did not create the "web of life," but humans are responsible for conserving a biological diversity. The Network makes this observation:
>
>> In the Web of Life, all animals and plants are interconnected into a complex scheme of ecological communities. Each organism can be thought of as an individual Web strand while ecological communities represent multiple strands. Biological diversity or biodiversity is essentially the scientific term that we apply to the Web of Life. ("Biodiversity")
>
> Because our future is inextricably bound to all other plants, animals, and resources, we are only harming ourselves when we bring harm to the diversity of the environment.

Citing Lines of Poetry

Incorporate short quotations of poetry (one or two lines) into your text. Use a slash with a space before and after to show line breaks.

> Part 3 of Eliot's "The Waste Land" (1922) remains a springtime search for nourishing water: "Sweet Thames, run softly, for I speak not loud or long" (line 176) says the speaker in "The Fire Sermon," while in Part 5 the speaker of "What the Thunder Said" yearns for "a damp gust / Bringing rain" (lines 394–95).

Set off three or more lines of poetry by indenting one inch or by centering the lines.

Citing Drama

Indent the dialogue of a play as a block. Begin with the character's name, indented one inch from the left margin and written in all capital letters. Follow the name with a period, tab forward and begin the quotation. Start a new line when the dialogue shifts to another character.

> At the end of *Oedipus Rex*, Kreon chastises Oedipus, reminding
> him that he no longer has control over his own life nor that of
> his children.
>
> KREON.   Come now and leave your children.
> OEDIPUS.   No! Do not take them from me!
> KREON.   Think no longerThat you are in command
>   here, rather thinkHow you served your own
>   destruction.

Changing Initial Capitals

In general, you should reproduce quoted materials exactly, yet one exception is permitted for logical reasons. Restrictive connectors, such as *that* or *because*, create restrictive clauses and eliminate a need for the comma.

> Another writer argues that "the single greatest impediment to
> our improving the lives of America's children is the myth that
> we are a child-oriented society" (Zigler 39).

Using Ellipsis Points to Omit Phrases

You may omit portions of quoted material with three spaced ellipsis points. In omitting material, do not change the meaning or take a quotation out of context.

Omission within a sentence. Three spaced ellipsis points (periods) signal omission from *within* a sentence:

> Phil Withim objects to the idea that "such episodes are
> intended to demonstrate that Vere . . . has the intelligence
> and insight to perceive the deeper issue" (118).

Omission at the end of a sentence. If an ellipsis occurs at the end of your sentence, use four periods with no space before the first or after the last. A closing quotation mark finishes the punctuation.

> Arnet and Jacques (10) declare that insects live in "all wild
> habitats as well as the full range of human environments. . . ."

However, if a page citation also appears at the end, use three periods with a space before each and put the sentence period after the final parenthesis.

> Arnet and Jacques declare that insects live in "all wild habitats as well as the full range of human environments . . . " (10).

Omission of complete sentences and paragraphs. Use a closing punctuation mark and three spaced ellipsis points when omitting one or more sentences from within a long quotation. This next example indicates the end of one sentence, the omission of one or more sentences, and a full sentence to end the passage.

> Foreman reminds us that parents of teenagers must use expertise to "sidestep hassling over nonsense . . . . You can let some things slide because you know she'll learn, as you did, by trial and error" (10–11).

Omission in poetry. If you omit a word or phrase in a quotation of poetry, use three or four ellipsis points just as you would with prose. If you omit a complete line or several lines, indicate the omission by a line of spaced periods that equals the average length of the line or lines.

> Do ye hear the children weeping, O my brothers,
> > Ere the sorrow comes with years?
> They are leaning their young heads against their mothers,
> > And <u>that</u> cannot stop their tears.
>
> . . . .
>
> They are weeping in the playtime of the others,
> In the country of the free. (Browning 382)

Using Brackets to Alter Quotations

Alter a quotation if necessary to emphasize a point or to make something clear. Within the brackets, add material, italicize an important word, or use the word *sic* (see below). Do not use parentheses within a quotation because parentheses must appear outside a quotation, as shown here:

> This same critic indicates that "we must avoid the temptation to read it [*The Scarlet Letter*] heretically" (118).

> "John F. Kennedy [was] an immortal figure of courage and dignity in the hearts of most Americans," notes one historian (Jones 82).

He says, for instance, that the "extended family is now rare in contemporary society, and with its demise the new parent has lost the <u>wisdom</u> [my emphasis] and daily support of older, more experienced family members" (Zigler 42).

Yearney says, "Theodore Roosevelt's final resting place in Hyde Park, New York [sic], is a quiet and humble plot when compared to his big game hunts in Africa or exploration in the Brazilian jungle" (113).

Theodore Roosevelt is buried in Oyster Bay, New York; Franklin D. Roosevelt is buried in Hyde Park, New York.

10c Writing the Works Cited References in MLA Style

The following examples show the correct MLA citation formats for books, periodicals, electronic sources, and other forms of information.

Works Cited Form—Books

Enter information for books in the following order:

1. Author(s)
2. Chapter or part of book
3. Title of the book
4. Editor, translator, or compiler
5. Edition
6. Volume number of book
7. Name of the series
8. Place, publisher, and date
9. Page numbers
10. Number of volumes
11. Medium of publication— "Print."

Items 1, 3, 8, and 11 are always required for print entries on the Works Cited page. Add other items according to the circumstances.

Armijo, Isidoro. "Sixty Minutes in Hell." *The Norton Anthology of Latino Literature*. Ed. Ilan Stavans. New York: Norton, 2011. 353–58. Print.

Following is a detailed breakdown of the components found in the previous entry:

Author Name. "Title for Section of the Book." *Book Title in Italics*. Name of the Editor. City, State of Publication: Name of Publisher, Year of Publication. Page Numbers. Medium of Publication.

Author

Moning, Karen Marie. *Into the Dreaming*. New York: Random House, 2012. Print.

Author, Anonymous

Bhagavad-Gita: The Song of God. Trans. Swami Prabhavananda
and Christopher Isherwood. New York: Penguin, 2012.
Print.

Authors, Two or Three

Baumeister, Roy F., and John Tierney. Willpower: Rediscovering
the Greatest Human Strength. New York: Penguin, 2012.
Print.

Authors, More Than Three

Use "et al.," which means "and others," or list all the authors.

Garrod, Andrew C., et al. Adolescent Portraits: Identity,
Relationships, and Challenges. 7th ed. Boston: Prentice
Hall, 2011. Print.

Orlich, Donald C., Robert J. Harder, Richard C. Callahan, Michael
S. Trevisan, and Abbie H. Brown. Teaching Strategies:
A Guide to Effective Instruction. Stamford, CT: Cengage,
2012. Print.

Author, Corporate or Institutional

A corporate author can be an association, a committee, or any group
or institution when the title page does not identify the names of the
members. List a committee or council as the author even when the
organization is also the publisher, as in this example:

American Medical Association. Health Professions Career and
Education Directory 2011–2012. 39th ed. New York:
Random, 2011. Print.

Author, Two or More Books by the Same Author

When an author has two or more works in the Works Cited list, do
not repeat his or her name with each entry. Rather, for the second
and additional entries, insert a continuous three-dash line flush with
the left margin, followed by a period. Also, list the works alphabetically by the title (ignoring *a, an,* and *the*), not by the year of publication. In the following example, the *B* of *Best* precedes the *L* of *Last*
and the *S* of *Safe*.

Sparks, Nicholas. The Best of Me. New York: Grand Central,
2011. Print.

---. The Last Song. New York: Grand Central, 2010. Print.

---. Safe Haven. New York: Grand Central, 2012. Print.

Anthology, Component Part

Provide the inclusive page numbers for the piece, not just the page or pages that you have cited in the text.

> Le Guin, Ursula K. "The Ones Who Walk Away from Omelas."
> *Literature: An Introduction to Fiction, Poetry, Drama, and Writing*. Eds. X. J. Kennedy and Dana Gioia. 11th ed. New York: Longman, 2011. 242–46. Print.

The Bible

Do not underscore or italicize the word "Bible" or the books of the Bible. Common editions need no publication information, but do underscore or italicize special editions of the Bible.

> The Bible. Print. [Denotes King James version]
> *The Geneva Bible*. 1560. Facsim. rpt. Madison: U of Wisconsin P, 1961. Print.
> *NIV [New International Version] Study Bible*. Personal Size Revised Edition. Grand Rapids, MI: Zondervan, 2011. Print.

Classical Works

> Homer. *The Odyssey*. Trans. William Cowper. Chula Vista: New Century, 2011. Print.

Cross-References to Works in a Collection

Cite several different selections from one anthology by giving a full reference to the anthology and abbreviated cross-references to the individual selections.

> Eggers, Dave, ed. *The Best American Nonrequired Reading*. Boston, Mariner, 2010. Print.
> Furuness, Bryan. "Man of Steel." Eggers 180–97.
> Keret, Etgar. "What, of This Goldfish, Would You Wish?" Eggers 262–67.
> Vonnegut, Kurt. "The Nice Little People." Eggers 431–38.

Dictionary, Encyclopedia, or Reference Book

Well-known works need only the edition and the year of publication. If no author is listed, begin with the title of the article:

> "Kiosk: Word History." *The American Heritage Dictionary of the English Language*. 5th ed. 2012. Print.
> Moran, Joseph. "Weather." *The World Book Encyclopedia*. 2009 ed. Print.

If you cite a specific definition from among several, add *Def.* (Definition), followed by the appropriate number/letter of the definition.

> "Level." Def. 4a. *The American Heritage Dictionary of the English Language.* 5th ed. 2012. Print.

Edition

Cite any edition beyond the first.

> Martini, Frederic H., Michael J. Timmons, and Robert B. Tallitsch. *Human Anatomy.* 7th ed. San Francisco: Benjamin Cummings, 2011. Print.

Editor, Translator, Illustrator, or Compiler

If the name of the editor or compiler appears on the title page of an anthology or compilation, place it first:

> Young, Kevin, and David Lehman, eds. *The Best American Poetry 2011.* New York: Scribner, 2012. Print.

Sourcebooks and Casebooks

> Ellmann, Richard. "Reality." *Yeats: The Man and the Masks.* New York: Macmillan, 1948. Rpt. in *Yeats: A Collection of Critical Essays.* Ed. John Unterecker. Twentieth Century Views. Englewood Cliffs: Prentice, 1963. 163–74. Print.

Title of a Book in Another Language

In general, use lowercase letters for foreign titles except for the first major word and proper names. Provide a translation in brackets if you think it necessary (e.g., *Étranger [The Stranger]* or Praha [Prague]).

> Allende, Isabel. *La isla bajo el mar.* New York: Knopf, 2010. Print.
>
> Coelho, Paulo. *El vencedor esta solo.* New York: HarperCollins, 2010. Print.

Volume

> Chircop, Aldo, S. Coffen-Smout, and Moira L. McConnell, eds. *Ocean Yearbook.* Vol. 26. Chicago: U of Chicago P, 2012. Print.

Works Cited Form—Periodicals

For journal or magazine articles, use the following order:

1. Author(s)
2. Title of the article
3. Name of the periodical
4. Series number (if it is relevant)
5. Volume number (for journals)
6. Issue number (if needed)
7. Date of publication
8. Page numbers
9. Medium of publication— "Print."

> Rafuse, Ethan S. "Generals We Love to Hate." *America's Civil War*. Jan. 2012: 30–37. Print.

Following is a detailed breakdown of the components found in the previous entry:

> Author's Name. "Title of Article." *Title of Periodical*. Publication Date: Page Numbers. Medium of Publication.

Abstract

If you cite from an abstract found in a journal, be sure to designate that you are citing only from the overview information found in the abstract.

> Gaillard, Thomas, and David A. Case. "Evaluation of DNA Force Fields in Implicit Solvation." Abstract. *Journal of Chemistry Theory and Computation* 7.10 (2011): 3181–98. Print.

Author

> Blagden, David W., Jack S. Levy, and William R. Thompson. "Sea Powers, Continental Powers, and Balancing Theory." *International Security* 36.2 (Fall 2011): 190–202. Print.

Author, Anonymous

> "Which Side Are You On?" *America's Civil War*. Nov. 2011: 19. Print.

Interview, Published

> Smith, Elly. Interview with Florence Welch. "Florence + The Machine." *Lab Magazine* July 2010: 11–15. Print.

Journal, with All Issues for a Year Paged Continuously

> Andreas, Peter. "Illicit Globalization: Myths, Misconceptions, and Historical Lessons." *Political Science Quarterly* 126.3 (2011): 406–25. Print.

Journal, with Each Issue Paged Anew

Add the issue number after the volume number and/or add the month.

> Bomer, Randy. "What Makes a Teaching Moment: Spheres of
>   Influence in Professional Activity." *English Journal.* 101.1
>   (Sept. 2011): 55–61. Print.

Magazine

Provide an exact date for magazines. There is no reason to list the volume and issue numbers.

> Toobin, Jeffrey. "Without a Paddle." *New Yorker* 27 Sept. 2010:
>   34–41. Print.

Supply inclusive page numbers (202–09, 85–115, 1112–24); however, if an article is paged in various places in the magazine, write only the first page number and a plus sign with no intervening space. Also, the month suffices for monthly and bimonthly publications:

> Fair, Jeff. "The Other Arctic." *Audubon* Nov./Dec. 2011: 82+.
>   Print.

Notes, Editorials, Queries, Reports, Comments, Letters

Identify the types of pieces that are not full-fledged articles.

> Bly, Adam. "Science in 2006." Comment. *SEED* 2.2 (Dec./Jan.
>   2006): 10. Print.
> Perina, Kaja. "The Double Life of Secrets." Editor's note.
>   *Psychology Today* Oct. 2010: 3. Print.

Review Article

Name the reviewer and the title of the review. Then write *Rev. of* and the title of the work being reviewed, followed by a comma, and the name of the author or producer.

> Grotta, Sally Wiener and Daniel Grotta. "Hi Ti's Pocket Studio
>   Printer." Rev. of Hi Ti Pocket Studio. *Shutterbug* Nov.
>   2010: 74+. Print.

If the name of reviewer is not provided, begin the entry with the title of the review.

> "Lighting Aids." Rev. of Reflector Kits. *Digital SLR Photography*
>   Sept. 2010: 127–31. Print.

Title within the Article's Title

> Brinkley, Alan. "From Theodore White to *Game Change*: A Review
> Essay." *Political Science Quarterly* 125.3 (Fall 2010):
> 493–503. Print.

Volume, Issue, and Page Numbers for Journals

Some journals are paged continuously through all issues of an entire year, so listing the month of publication is unnecessary. For clarity, provide the volume and issue number, as well as the page numbers. Give the issue number following the volume number, separated by a period.

> Gottdiener, William H. "Improving the Relationship Between
> the Randomized Clinical Trial and Real-World Clinical
> Practice." *Psychotherapy* 48.3 (Sept. 2011): 231–33. Print.

Works Cited Form—Newspapers

Provide the name of the author; the title of the article; the name of the newspaper as it appears on the masthead, omitting any introductory article (e.g., *Wall Street Journal*, not *The Wall Street Journal*); and the complete date—day, month (abbreviated), and year. Omit any volume and issue numbers. Provide a page number as listed (e.g., 21, B-6, 14C, D3).

> Parr-Moody, Karen. "A Walk Down (Not So Haunted) Memory
> Lane." *Leaf Chronicle* [Clarksville, TN] 30 Oct. 2011: D1.
> Print.

In the case of locally published newspapers, add the city in square brackets (see the sample entry immediately above). Following is a detailed breakdown of the components found in the entry above:

> Author's Name. "Title of Article." *Title of Newspaper*. Publication
> Date: Page Number. Medium of Publication.

Newspaper in One Section

> McTague, Jim. "A GOP House?" *Barron's* 27 Sept. 2010: 27–29.
> Print.

Newspaper with Sections

> Griffin, Greg. "Forecast Getting Gloomier." *Denver Post* 12 Oct.
> 2010: 1A+. Print.

Newspaper Editorial with No Author Listed

> "Soldier Defines Heroism." Editorial. *[Nashville] Tennessean*
> 15 Sept. 2010: A16. Print.

Newspaper Column, Cartoon, Comic Strip, or Advertisement

Add a description to the entry to explain that the citation refers to something other than a regular news story.

> Robinson, Eugene. "The Spoiled-brat American Electorate."
>   Column. *Washington Post* 3 Sept. 2010: A3. Print.

Works Cited Form—Government Documents

As a general rule, place information in the bibliographic entry in this order: Government, Body or agency, Subsidiary body, Title of document, Identifying numbers, Publication facts. When you cite two or more works by the same government, substitute three hyphens for the name of each government or body that you repeat:

> United States. Cong. House.
> ---. ---. Senate.
> ---. Dept. of Justice.

Congressional Papers

Senate and House sections are identified by an S or an H with document numbers (e.g., S. Res. 16) and page numbers (e.g., H2345-47).

> United States. Cong. House. Small Business Jobs and Credit Act
>   of 2010. 111th Cong., 1st sess. H. Bill 5297. Washington,
>   DC: GPO, 2010. Print.
> ---. ---. ---. Continuing Appropriations Act, 2011. 111th Cong.,
>   1st sess. H. Bill 3081. Washington, DC: GPO, 2010. Print.

If you provide a citation to the *Congressional Record*, you should abbreviate it and provide only the date and page numbers.

> *Cong. Rec.* 1 Oct. 2010: S1050-54. Print.

Executive Branch Documents

> United States. Dept. of State. *Foreign Relations of the United*
>   *States: Diplomatic Papers, 1943.* 5 vols. Washington, DC:
>   GPO, 1943–44. Print.
> ----. President. *2012 Economic Report of the President.*
>   Washington, DC: GPO, 2012. Print.

Documents of State Governments

Publication information on state papers will vary widely, so provide sufficient data for your reader to find the document.

2010–2011 Statistical Report. Nashville: Tennessee Board
of Regents, 2011. TBR A-001-03. Print.

Tennessee Election Returns, 1796–1825. Microfilm. Nashville:
Tennessee State Library and Archives, n.d. M-Film JK 5292
T46. Print.

"Giles County." *2011–12 Directory of Public Schools.* Nashville:
State Dept. of Educ., 2012. 61. Print.

Legal Citations and Public Statutes

Use the following examples as guidelines for developing your citations, which can usually appear as parenthetical citations in your text,
but not on the Works Cited page.

Illinois. Silent Reflection and Student Prayer Act. Sec. 105
ILCS 20/) 2010. Print.

Noise Control Act of 2012. Pub. L. 92-574. 2012. Stat. 86.
Print.

State v. Lane. Minnesota 263 N. W. 608. 1935. Print.

Works Cited Form—Internet Sources

Include these items as appropriate to the source:

1. Author/editor name
2. Title of the article within quotation marks
3. Publication information
4. Date and description for government documents
5. Name of the sponsoring institution or organization, if available
6. Website posting date
7. Medium of publication—"Web."
8. Date of your access, followed by a comma or period

Bellis, Mary. "The History of the Atomic Bomb and the
Manhattan Project." *About: Inventors.* 2012. Web. 13
May 2012.

Abstract

Quinn, Patrick D., Cynthia A. Stappenbeck, and Kim Fromme.
"Collegiate Heavy Drinking Prospectively Predicts Change
in Sensation Seeking and Impulsivity." Abstract. *Journal
of Abnormal Psychology* 120.3 (2011). 528–43. Web.
22 Feb. 2012.

Anonymous Article

"Child Passenger Safety." National Highway Traffic Safety
Administration. 2012. Web. 11 Apr. 2012.

Archive or Scholarly Project

Victorian Women Writers Project. Indiana U Digital Library
Program. 2010. Web. 19 Apr. 2011.

Article from an Online Magazine

Magnani, Lorenzo. "Building Artificial Mimetic Minds: How
Hybrid Humans Make Up Distributed Cognitive Systems."
APA Online. American Psychological Association, Spring
2010. Web. 19 Nov. 2010.

Article from a Scholarly Journal

Jacob, Theodore, et al. "Course of Alcohol Dependence Among
Vietnam Combat Veterans and Nonveteran Controls."
Journal of Studies on Alcohol and Drugs 71.5 (2010):
629–39. Web. 12 Feb. 2011.

Blogs and Chat Rooms

Chat rooms seldom have great value, but on occasion you might find
something that you wish to cite; if so, use this form:

Bursack, Carol Bradley, narr. "Calling Elders by Preferred Name
Is Important to Caregiving Bond." *Minding Our Elders Blog,*
12 Oct. 2010. Web. 28 Oct. 2010.

Chapter or Portion of a Book

Place the chapter title after the author's name:

Dewey, John. "Waste in Education." *The School and Society*.
Chicago: U of Chicago P, 1907. Web. 4 Mar. 2012.

E-mail

Wright, Ellen. "Online Composition Courses." Message to the
author. 24 May 2011. E-mail.

Encyclopedia Article Online

"Kurt Vonnegut, Jr." *Encyclopedia Britannica Online*.
Encyclopedia Britannica, 2011. Web. 9 Mar. 2012.

Film or Video Online

"Epiphany: Festival of Lights." *Greek Orthodox Archdiocese of
America*. Leadership 100, 2010. Web. 8 Jan. 2011.

Journal Article

Castellanos, Kenia M., et al. "Does Exposure to Ambient Odors Influence the Emotional Content of Memories?" *American Journal of Psychology*. 123.3 (Fall 2010): Web. 22 Jan. 2011.

Newsletter

Meagher, Sharon M. "Pushing the Boundaries of Philosophy." *APA Online.* American Psychological Association, 9.2 (Spring 2010). Web. 30 Sept. 2010.

Newspaper Article, Column, Editorial

Forker, Jennifer. "Go Local for Affordable Works by Others." *Miamiherald.com*. Miami Herald, 13 Oct. 2010. Web. 13 Oct. 2010.

Novel

Conrad, Joseph. "Chapter 1." *Heart of Darkness.* 1902. Web. 26 Apr. 2012.

Online Posting for E-mail Discussion Groups

Supply the name of the list's moderator as well as the Internet site if known; otherwise show the e-mail address of the list's moderator.

Colthart, Bruce. "You Have to Ask for the Work to Get The Work." Online Posting. *Design Democracy*, 9 Oct. 2010. Web. 16 Oct. 2010.

Poem, Song, or Story

Hardy, Thomas. "Her Death and After." *Wessex Poems and Other Verses*. 1898. *Bartleby.com*. Great Books Online, 2011. Web. 10 May 2011.

Television, Radio, or Sound Clip Recording

Kissack, Andrea. "In Search of Charging Stations for Electric Cars." *Morning Edition*. National Public Radio, 12 Oct. 2010. Web. 14 Oct. 2010.

University Posting, Online Article

Goodman, Herb. "Learning Transcends the Classroom." Online Posting. Eastern Kentucky U, 23 Aug. 2010. Web. 13 Oct. 2011.

Website

Robert Penn Warren: 1905–1989. Web. 15 Mar. 2012.

Works Cited Form—Databases

Most libraries have converted their computer searches to online databases, such as Gale Cengage (InfoTrac), EBSCOhost, Electric Library, and others. Omit the identifying numbers for the database or the key term used in the search. Following are examples:

> "America's Children: Key National Indicators of Well-Being,
>   2010." Federal Interagency Forum on Child and Family
>   Statistics. July 2010. *ERIC*. Web. 8 Dec. 2010.
> Esslin, Martin. "Theater of the Absurd." *Grolier Multimedia*
>   *Encyclopedia*. 2011 ed. Web. 22 Oct. 2011.
> Pearce, Colin D. "The Metaphysical Federalism of William
>   Gilmore Simms." *Studies in the Literary Imagination* 42.1
>   (2010): 121–40. *InfoTrac*. Web. 19 Sept. 2011.
> Crawford, Stephanie. "10 Common Skin Irritants." *Discovery*
>   *Health* 2011. *EBSCOhost*. Web. 23 Jan. 2011.

On rare occasions you may access online material in the library that has no URL or the URL on your printout is scrambled or incomplete. In such a case, make a citation to the source, then give the name of the database, italicized (if known); the name of the service; the library; the medium of publication; and the date of access.

> Boyer, Wanda. "Preadolescent Violence Among Girls." *Youth*
>   *and Society* 42.1 (Sept. 2010): 33–58. *MasterFILE Elite*.
>   Clarksville Montgomery County Library, Clarksville, TN.
>   Web. 23 Feb. 2011.

Works Cited Form—Other Sources
Artwork

> "Modern Life: Edward Hopper and His Life." Whitney Museum of
>   American Art, New York. 28 Feb. 2011. Visual art.

Use this next form to cite reproductions in books and journals.

> Raphael. *School of Athens*. The Vatican, Rome. *The World*
>   *Book-Encyclopedia*, 2010 ed. Print.

Broadcast Interview

> Henry, Ed. "The Stakeout." Interview. CNN. Cable News
>   Network, 12 Oct. 2010. Television.

Film, Videocassette, or DVD

Cite the title of a film, the director, the distributor, and the year of release.

The Adjustment Bureau. Dir. George Nolfi. Universal Video, 2011. DVD.

Crimmins, Morton. "Robert Lowell—American Poet." Lecture. Western State U, 2011. Videocassette.

Manuscript (MS.) and Typescript (TS.)

Moss, Millicent. Journal 3, MS. Millicent Moss Private Papers, Emporia, KS. 2012.

Williams, Ralph. "Walking on the Water." 2011. TS.

Pamphlet

Treat pamphlets as you would a book.

Federal Reserve Board. *Consumer Handbook to Credit Protection Laws*. Washington, DC: GPO, 2012. Print.

Performance

Treat a performance (e.g., play, opera, ballet, or concert) as you would a film, but include the site (normally the theater and city) and the date of the performance.

Under the Cherokee Moon. Cherokee Heritage Center, Tahlequah, OK. 21 Aug. 2010. Performance.

Public Address or Lecture

McDonald, David. "Finding Immigrant Ancestors." St. Louis Genealogical Soc., St. Louis. 23 Oct. 2010. Address.

Recording on Record, Tape, or Disk

If you are not citing a compact disc, indicate the medium (e.g., audio-cassette, audiotape [reel-to-reel tape], or LP [long-playing record]).

"Chaucer: The Nun's Priest's Tale." *Canterbury Tales*. Narr. in Middle English by Alex Edmonds. London, 2005. Audiocassette.

Table, Illustration, Chart, or Graph

Tables or illustrations of any kind published within works need a detailed label (chart, table, figure, photograph, and so on):

"Early Childhood Education Assembly." Figure. *English Journal* 101.1 (Sept. 2011): 124. Print.

Television or Radio Program

God in America. 3 episodes. American Experience. Dir. David Belton. NPT, Nashville. 11 Oct. 2010. Television.

Formatting the Paper in MLA Style

The format of a research paper consists of the following parts. It is essential that you have a title, body of the paper, and a Works Cited page.

1. Title page or opening page with title
2. Outline
3. The text of the paper
4. Content notes
5. Appendix
6. Works Cited

Title Page or Opening Page

A research paper in MLA style does not need a separate title page unless you include an outline, abstract, or other introductory matter. See page 150 for an example.

Outline

Include your outline with the finished manuscript only if your instructor requires it.

The Text of the Paper

Double-space your entire paper. In general, you should *not* use subtitles or numbered divisions for your paper, even if it becomes twenty pages long. Do not start "Notes" or "Works Cited" on the final page of text.

Content Endnotes Page

Label this page with the word "Notes" centered at the top edge of the sheet, at least one double-space below your page numbering sequence in the upper-right corner. Double-space between the "Notes" heading and the first note. Number the notes in sequence with raised superscript numerals to match those within your text. Double-space all entries and double-space between them.

Appendix

Place additional material, if necessary, in an appendix that precedes the Works Cited page. This is the logical location for tables and illustrations, computer data, questionnaire results, complicated statistics, mathematical proofs, or detailed descriptions of special equipment.

Works Cited

Center the heading "Works Cited" one inch from the top edge of the sheet. Continue the page numbering sequence in the upper-right corner. Double-space throughout. Use hanging indention—that is, set the first line of each entry flush left and indent subsequent lines five spaces or one-half inch. Alphabetize by the last name of the author. See page 154, the sample student paper in Section 10e, for an example.

10e Writing a Literary Paper in MLA Style

Sample Research Paper

The sample research paper demonstrates the form and style of a literary research paper written to the specifications of the MLA style. Annotations in the margins explain elements of style that may be important in the development of your paper.

Murphy 1

Anthony Murphy

English 2202

Dr. Pasch

March 21, 2012

Wilfred Owen—Battlefront Poet

Murphy opens with background information.

In the summer of 1917, World War I was at its peak. Countries were being torn apart, men were being slaughtered by the thousands, and the civilians were starving. But out of the mists of this carnage came one of the greatest war poets of the twentieth century. With his horrific imagery and anti-war themes, readers learned the darker side of war. Although short lived, the poems of Wilfred Owen introduced readers around the world to the realization that war has its consequences.

Murphy establishes the concept he will explore.

Born in March 1893 in a house near Oswestry, England, Wilfred Owen spent most of his childhood reading the scriptures and learning the ways of the church. As a committed Christian and with a "pious mother . . . [urging] him to become an Anglican priest," according to Rich Geib, Owen seriously considered entering the ministry. Instead he decided to attend the University of London, where unfortunately he was denied a scholarship and therefore had to work as a reverend's liaison to pay his tuition. By the age of nineteen, Owen had already engrossed himself into poetry, being especially impressed with Keats and Shelley (Roberts). After a few years of college, he made his way to Bordeaux, France to work as a private tutor at the Berlitz School. It was here that Owen first received word that war had broke out between the European nations.

During the first year, Owen was a frequent visitor of soldiers who had been wounded during battle. After being pressured by what he saw in the hospitals, and the guilt that ensued by the national propaganda, Owen was enticed into joining the military (Roberts; Geib). In the fall of 1915, Owen left France and headed to England to enlist in the Army. In June he was commissioned a second lieutenant and made a brief statement at his commissioning: "I came out in order to help these boys—directly by leading them as well as an officer can" (qtd. in Geib). After Owen's commission, he was given a platoon under the Manchester division which in January 1917 was sent to the trenches of France. It was these first days of battle "where his outlook on life changed permanently" (Geib). For months he dodged bullets and bombs, only to see his men be killed daily. In April, Owen's luck ran out, and his trench was hit with a stream of explosions. Suffering from shell-shock, he was evacuated to Craiglockhart War Hospital. It was here that Owen would meet the inspiration to his destiny.

Siegfried Sassoon was already an acclaimed poet when Owen met him. Sassoon was a mentor to Owen and introduced him to figures such as Robert Graves and H. G. Wells ("Wilfred Owen"). Sassoon also assisted Owen in his writings of "Anthem for Doomed Youth," and "Dulce et Decorum Est." With the assistance of Sassoon, Owen spent the next several months developing and writing his poetry. His insight and firsthand experience brought to

Murphy cites the authorities on Owen in brief but effective ways.

prominence the "British trench poets and their literary art" (Lusty 199). From these experiences, according to Parker and Kermode, Owen took as his subject "the pity of war" by detailing the "passive suffering of the individual soldier, often with homoerotic intensity" (570). In June 1918, Owen was sent back to the lines to join his regiment, but not before completing numerous poems. As noted by Stephanie Fishwick, it was here at Craiglockhart where "[Owen] wrote many of the poems for which he is remembered today."

Owen rejoined the 2nd Manchester Regiment in Scarborough, and was immediately sent back to France. In October, as the Great War was coming to an end, Owen's unit was still on the offensive (Fishwick). As Owen's men entered the town of Amien, they were attacked by a German machine gun. Owen advanced the German position and defeated the enemy single handedly. Due to his heroic acts he was awarded the Military Cross for Bravery (Fishwick). On November 11, 1918, the Armistice was signed and World War One had officially ended. People all over the world were cheering and celebrating, including the parents of Wilfred Owen. But on the afternoon of that day Owen's parents received a telegram informing them that their son had been killed just seven days prior.

"It was only when the war and his life came to an end that his poetry was truly recognized," ("Examine"). After two years, Owen's poems were finally published, thanks to the work of his mentor Siegfried Sassoon. In December 1920, Sassoon published a book called *Poems of Wilfred Owen* which consisted of ten of Owen's best poems with each poem introduced by Sassoon (Geib). One poem that was not put into the book was "Disabled." "'Disabled' presents a poignant picture of a young soldier 'legless, sewn short at elbow' . . . and shows what he had been before against what he is left with," writes Meg Crane of the Wilfred Owen Association.

Murphy 4

> He sat in a wheeled chair, waiting for dark,
> And shivered in his ghastly suit of grey,
> Legless, sewn short at elbow. Through the park
> Voices of boys rang saddening like a hymn,
> Voices of play and pleasure after day,
> Till gathering sleep had mothered them from him. (l.1–5)

Lines of the poem are identified, line breaks are maintained, and the line numbers are listed.

"Disabled" is a perfect example of Owen's anti-war feelings. There is a sense of negativity just from the title alone (Fishwick). The character in the story is never given a name, which adds a feeling of worthlessness to his life ("Examine"). The poem further relates how the soldier only went to war to impress the girls, and now all people do is pity him rather than thank him. The soldier never really wanted to go to war, but pressure led him to do so. Paul Groves describes the pressure by stating, "the soldier was already a football hero . . . and now the soldier must become a war hero as well." The poem was written not only to give pity for these soldiers, but to reflect the personal conflict Owen had with his enlistment. "Disabled" shows that people have different reasons for going to war and illustrates the effects that war has on men, both mentally and physically (Groves). The overall message of "Disabled" however, is do not let others dictate your life.

This section demonstrates the manner in which Murphy interprets one of the poems, citing from it and explaining the implications in light of the poetic theme.

With the signing of the Armistice, peace was finally realized for a brief period of time. Wilfred Owen opened the minds of many readers after the war by showing that soldiers just do not sign up willingly and that battle during or after war is never glorious. Moreover, his poetry "made the Great War's truthtelling norm" (Bradbury 220). Through "poetic expression under ideological pressure in times of war," he gives a stirring look at the grotesque, brutal reality of combat (Norris 136). Although he is gone, Wilfred Owen's life lives on through the poems he left the world— "My subject is War, and the pity of War. The Poetry is in the pity" (qtd. Geib).

Murphy 5

Works Cited

Bradbury, Malcolm, ed. *The Atlas of Literature*. New York:
  Stewart, Tabori, & Chang, 1998. Print.

Crane, Meg, ed. "Disabled." Wilfred Owen Association.
  2012. Web. 19 Mar. 2012.

"Examine the Way Three Poems by Wilfred Owen Depict the
  Horror of War." Coursework Help. 2012. Web. 18 Mar.
  2012.

Fishwick, Stephanie. "The Wilfred Owen Collection." The
  First World War Poetry Digital Archive. 2012. Web.
  13 Mar. 2012.

Geib, Rich. "Wilfred Owen (1893–1918) Poet, Patriot,
  Soldier, Pacifist." Rich Geib's Universe. 2012. Web.
  15 Mar. 2012.

Groves, Paul. "Biography Wilfred Owen." 2007. Web.
  17 Mar. 2012.

Lusty, Heather. "Shaping the National Voice: Poetry of
  WWI." *Journal of Modern Literture*. 30.1 (Fall 2006):
  199–209. Print.

Norris, Margot. "Teaching World War I Poetry—Comparatively."
  College Literature. 32.3 (Summer 2005): 136–53. Print.

Parker, Peter, and Frank Kermode, eds. *A Reader's Guide to
  Twentieth-Century Writers*. New York: Oxford UP, 1996.
  Print.

Roberts, David. "Wilfred Owen: Greatest War Poet in the
  English Language (1893–1918)." Web. 14 Mar. 2012.

"Wilfred Owen." Academy of American Poets. 2012. Web.
  17 Mar. 2012.

Citation for a book.

Citation to a website.

Citation for a journal entry.

11

Writing in APA Style

Clear Targets

You may need to write a research paper in a style that features the authority's name and the year of publication. American Psychological Association style (APA) has gained wide acceptance in the social sciences, and versions similar to it are used in the biological sciences, business, and the earth sciences. The following components discussed in this chapter will help to document the references used in your research paper:

- Establishing a critical approach for the assignment
- Writing in the proper tense for an APA-styled paper
- Blending sources into your writing
- Preparing the list of references
- Formatting a paper in APA style

The APA documentation style gives all scholars in the social sciences a consistent way to consult the sources that are cited in your project.

11a Meeting the Demands of the Assignment

In the social sciences, your assignment is likely to be a:

- Theoretical article
- Report of empirical research
- Review article

Writing Theoretical Articles

A theory paper draws on existing research to trace the development of a theory or to compare theories. Your theoretical analysis will examine the current thinking about social topics, such as criminal behavior, dysfunctional families, and learning disorders. The theory paper generally accomplishes four things:

1. Identifies a problem or hypothesis that has historical implications in the scientific community

2. Traces the development and history of the evolution of the theory
3. Provides a systematic analysis of the articles that have explored the problem
4. Arrives at a judgment and discussion of the prevailing theory

Reporting on Empirical Research

When you conduct original research in the field or lab, you should provide a report that details your procedures and findings. The report also may take the form of a proposal to explain your hypothesis and the manner in which you will conduct the study. See pages 58–60 for the discussion of observation, testing, and other methods for conducting the research. Typically, an empirical study:

1. Introduces the problem or hypothesis under investigation and explains the purpose of the work
2. Describes the design and methodology of the research
3. Reports the results of the investigation or test
4. Discusses, interprets, and explores the implications of the findings

Reviewing Articles and Books

A common assignment in some courses is a paper in which you make a critical evaluation of a published article or book, or a set of articles on a common topic. Its purpose is to examine the state of current research to determine, in part, if additional work might be in order. It serves several purposes:

1. Defines the problem to clarify the hypothesis
2. Summarizes the article or book under review
3. Analyzes the literature to discover strengths, weaknesses, and/ or inconsistencies in the research
4. Recommends additional research that might grow logically from the work under review

(See pages 101–108 for an example of a review of literature.)

Establishing a Critical Approach

In scientific writing, the thesis statement (see pages 8–11) usually appears as a hypothesis, statement of principle, or enthymeme.

The *hypothesis* is a theory that needs testing and analysis, which you will do during your research. It is an idea expressed as a truth for the purpose of argument and investigation and testing. Put another way, it makes a prediction based upon a theory.

> It was predicted that patients who suffer a compulsive bulimia disorder would have a more disrupted family life.

In similar fashion, the *statement of principle* makes a declarative statement in defense of an underlying but unstated theory. This report attempts to prove the hypothetical principle on the basis of testing, observation, interviews, and other methods of field research, as explained on pages 55–60.

> The most effective recall cue is the one that is encoded within the event that is to be remembered.

11c Writing in the Proper Tense for an APA-Styled Paper

APA style requires that you use the past tense or the present perfect tense ("Marshall *stipulated*" or "the work of Elmford and Mills *has demonstrated*"). APA style does require present tense when you discuss the results of your research (e.g., *"the results confirm"* or *"the study indicates"*) and when you mention established knowledge (e.g., *"the therapy offers some hope"* or *"salt contributes to hypertension"*). The next sentence uses tense correctly for APA style:

> The danger of steroid use exists for every age group, even youngsters. Lloyd and Mercer (2012) reported on six incidents of liver damage to 14-year-old swimmers who used steroids.

11d Blending Sources into Your Writing

APA style uses these conventions for in-text citations:

- Last names only
- The year, within parentheses, immediately after the name of the author
- Page numbers with a direct quotation, seldom with a paraphrase
- Uses "p." or "pp." before page numbers

> Montague (2012) advanced the idea of combining the social sciences and mathematics to chart human behavior.

One study advanced the idea of combining the social sciences and mathematics to chart human behavior (Montague, 2012).

Montague (2012) has advanced the idea of "soft mathematics," which is the practice of "applying mathematics to study people's behavior" (p. B4).

Citing a Block of Material

Present a quotation of forty words or more as a separate block, indented five spaces or 1/2 inch from the left margin. Do not enclose it within quotation marks. Set parenthetical citations outside the last period.

> Albert (2011) reported the following:
>
> Whenever these pathogenic organisms attack the human body and begin to multiply, the infection is set in motion. The host responds to this parasitic invasion with efforts to cleanse itself of the invading agents. When rejection efforts of the host become visible (fever, sneezing, congestion), the disease status exists. (pp. 314–315)

Citing a Work with More Than One Author

When one work has two or more authors, use *and* in the text but use *&* in the citation.

Werner and Throckmorton (2012) offered statistics on the toxic levels of water samples from six rivers.

It was reported (Werner & Throckmorton, 2012) that toxic levels exceeded the maximum allowed each year since 1995.

For three to five authors, name them all in the first entry [e.g., Torgerson, Andrews, Smith, Lawrence, & Dunlap (2011)], but thereafter use "et al." [e.g., (Torgerson et al., 2011)]. For six or more authors, employ "et al." in the first and in all subsequent instances [e.g., (Fredericks et al., 2012)].

Citing More Than One Work by an Author

Use small letters (a, b, c) to identify two or more works published in the same year by the same author, for example, (Thompson, 2012a) and (Thompson, 2012b). Then use "2012a" and "2012b" in your list of references. If necessary, specify additional information:

Horton (2012; cf. Thomas, 2011a, p. 89, and 2011b, p. 426) suggested an intercorrelation of these testing devices. But after multiple-group analysis, Welston (2011, esp. p. 211) reached an opposite conclusion.

Citing Indirect Sources

Use a double reference to cite somebody who has been quoted in a book or article.

In other research, Massie and Rosenthal (2010) studied home movies of children diagnosed with autism, but determining criteria was difficult due to the differences in quality and dating of the available videotapes (cited in Osterling & Dawson, 2011, p. 248).

Abbreviating Corporate Authors in the Text

Corporate authors may be abbreviated after the initial full reference:

One source has questioned the results of the use of aspirin for arthritis treatment in children (American Medical Association [AMA], 2012).

Thereafter, refer to the corporate author by initials: (AMA, 2012).

Citing an Anonymous Author

When a work has no author listed, cite the title.

The cost per individual student has continued to rise rapidly ("Money Concerns," 2012, p. 2).

Citing Electronic Sources

In general, omit page numbers for articles you find on the Internet. However, if an online article shows original numbering, by all means supply that information in your citation (Jones, 2012, para. 5).

The most common type of diabetes is non-insulin-dependent diabetes mellitus (NIDDM), which "affects 90% of those with diabetes and usually appears after age 40" (Larson, 2011, para. 3).

Abstract

"Psychologically oriented techniques used to elicit confessions may undermine their validity" (Kassin, 2011, abstract).

Online Magazine

BusinessWeek Online (2010) reported that peer-to-peer
computing is a precursor to new web applications.

E-mail

Personal communications, which others cannot retrieve, should be
cited in the text only and not mentioned at all on the References
page.

CDs, DVDs, Individual Discs

Encyclopedia Britannica (2011) has explained that the Abolition
Society, which originated in England in 1787, appears to be the
first organized group in opposition to slavery. Later, in 1823
the Anti-Slavery Society was formed by Thomas Fowell Buxton,
who wielded power as a member of Parliament.

11e   Preparing the List of References

Use the title "References" for your bibliography page. Alphabetize the
entries and double-space throughout. Every reference used in your
text should appear in your alphabetical list of references at the end of
the paper. Use the hanging indent format—that is, set the first line of
each entry flush left, and indent succeeding lines five spaces. Italicize
or underscore names of books, periodicals, and volume numbers,
including associated punctuation marks.

Enter information for books in the following order:

1. Author(s)' Last Name, Initials
2. Year of publication in parentheses
3. Chapter or part of book
4. Title of the book
5. Editor, translator, or compiler
6. Edition
7. Volume number of book
8. Name of the series
9. Place and publisher
10. Number of volumes

Items 1, 2, 3, and 8 are always required book entries on the
References list. Add other items according to the circumstances.

Grann, D. (2012). *The devil and Sherlock Holmes: Tales of murder,
madness, and obsession.* New York, NY: Knopf Doubleday.

Following is a detailed breakdown of the components found in
the previous entry:

Author Name. (Year of Publication). *Book title in italics.* City of publication, State: Name of Publisher.

References Form—Books

Massie, R. K. (2012). *Catherine the Great: Portrait of a woman.* New York, NY: Random House.

List chronologically, not alphabetically, two or more works by the same author. For example, Massie's 2007 publication would precede the 2012 publication.

Part of a Book

List author(s), date, chapter or section title, editor (with name in normal order) preceded by *In* and followed by (*Ed.*) or (*Eds.*), the name of the book (underscored or italicized), page numbers to the specific section of the book cited (placed with parentheses), place of publication, and publisher.

Litt, T. (2008). The monster. In Z. Smith (Ed.), *The book of other people* (pp. 133–138). New York, NY: Penguin.

If no author is listed, begin with the title of the article.

Mount of Olives. (2011). *Holman concise Bible dictionary.* Nashville, TN: B & H.

Encyclopedia or Dictionary

Downes, J., & Goodman, J. E. (2010). *Dictionary of finance and investment terms* (8th ed.). New York, NY: Barrons.

Moran, J. M. (2010). Weather. *World Book encyclopedia* (2010 ed., Vol. 21, pp. 156–171). Chicago, IL: World Book.

Book with Corporate Author

American Medical Association. (2012). *Current procedural terminology 2012.* Chicago, IL: AMA.

References Form—Periodicals

List author(s), year, title of the article without quotation marks and with only the first word (and any proper nouns) capitalized, name of the journal underscored or italicized and with all major words capitalized, volume number underscored or italicized, inclusive page numbers *not* preceded by "p." or "pp."

For journal or magazine articles, use the following order:

1. Author(s)' Last Name, Initials
2. Year of publication in parentheses
3. Title of article without quotation marks
4. Name of periodical
5. Series number (if it is relevant)
6. Volume number (for journals)
7. Issue number (if needed)
8. Page numbers

Possamai, A., & Lee, M. (2011). Hyper-real religions: Fear, anxiety and late-modern religious innovation. *Journal of Sociology, 47*(3), 227–242.

Following is a detailed breakdown of the components found in the previous entry:

Author Name(s). (Year of publication). Article title. Name of periodical, Volume number(Issue number), Page numbers.

Article in a Journal

Mather, M., & Knight, M. (2005). Goal-directed memory: The role of cognitive control in older adults' emotional memory. *Psychology and Aging, 20*(4), 554–570.

Article Retrieved from a Database

Loto, M. A. (2011). Impact of government sectoral expenditure on economic growth. *Journal of Economics and International Finance, 3*(11), 646–652. Retrieved from EBSCOhost database.

Article in a Magazine

Stutz, B. (2011, November/December). Walking with Wordsworth. *Audubon,* pp. 44–52.

Soodalter, R. (2012, January). Sing a song of war. *America's Civil War, 24*(6), 24–25.

Note: Show the volume number if it is available. If no volume number is given, use "p." or "pp." before giving the page numbers.

Article in a Newspaper

Meyer, J. P. (2011, November 2). Tax hikes stopped dead in their tracks. *Denver Post,* pp. A1+.

Abstract as the Cited Source

> Minton, M. S., & Mack, R. N. (2010, October). Naturalization of plant populations: The role of cultivation and population size and density [Abstract]. *Oecologia, 164*, 399–409.

Review

> Biswas, B. (2010). Hierarchy in international relations. [Rev. article]. *Political Science Quarterly, 125*, 513–514.

Report

> Gorman, L. (2011). *Reporting insurance fraud* (No. 2011–1). Hartford, CT: Insurance Institute.

References Form—Nonprint Material

Computer Program

> Excel 2011. (2011). [Computer software]. Redmond, WA: Microsoft.

DVD, Videotape, Film

> Edwards, B. (Director). (1961). *Breakfast at Tiffany's.* [DVD]. Hollywood, CA: Paramount.

Interviews, Letters, and Memos

> Barstow, I. (2012, April 22). Palm reading as prediction [Interview]. Chattanooga, TN.

References Form—Internet Sources

The following information conforms to the instructions of APA. When citing sources in the References of your APA-style paper, provide this information if available:

1. Author/editor last name, followed by a comma, the initials, and a period
2. Year of publication, followed by a comma, then month and day for magazines and newspapers, within parentheses, followed by a period
3. Title of the article, not within quotations and not italicized, with the first word and proper nouns capitalized. *Note:* This is also the place to describe the work within brackets, as with [Abstract] or [Letter to the editor].

4. Name of the book, journal, or complete work, underscored or italicized, if one is listed
5. Volume number, if listed, underscored or italicized
6. Page numbers only if you have that data from a printed version of the journal or magazine. If the periodical has no volume number, use "p." or "pp." before the numbers; if the journal has a volume number, omit "p." or "pp."
7. Give the DOI (Digital Object Identifier) if available
8. If no DOI is available, use the words "Retrieved from" followed by the URL. Line breaks in URLs should come before punctuation marks such as slashes.

Article from an Online Journal

Patterson, N., & Sears, C.A. (2011, Spring). Letting men off the hook? *Genders*. Retrieved from http://www.genders.org /g53/g53_patterson_sears.html

Article with DOI Assigned

Nickson, D., & Korczynski, M. (2009). Aesthetic labour, emotional labour and masculinity [Editorial]. *Gender, Work and Organization, 16(3)*, 291–299. doi:10.1111/j.1468-0432.2009.00445.x

Article from a Printed Journal, Reproduced Online

Many articles online are the exact duplicates of their printed versions, so if you view an article in its electronic form and are confident that the electronic form is identical to the printed version, add within brackets the words *Electronic version*. This allows you to omit the URL.

Bechtel, W. (2010). Mechanism and biological explanation. [Electronic version]. *Philosophy of Science, 78(4)*, 533–557.

Add the URL and date of access if page numbers are not indicated.

Allen, M. (2011, November). Building better fishing. *Missouri Conservationist, 72(11)*. Retrieved from http://mdc .mo.gov/conmag/2011/11/building-better-fishing

Abstract

LaGrange, B., et al. (2011). Disentangling the prospective relations between maladaptive cognitions and depressive symptoms. [Abstract]. *Journal of Abnormal Psychology, 120(3)*. Retrieved from http://psycnet.apa.org/journals /abn/120/3/511/

Article from a Database

University libraries, as well as public libraries, feature servers that supply articles in large databases, such as PsycInfo, ERIC, netLibrary, and others. If readily available, include the item number within parentheses. You need not cite the URL. If you cite only from an abstract, mention that fact in your reference entry.

America's children: Key national indicators of well-being.
(2011). Federal Interagency Forum on Child and Family
Statistics. Retrieved from ERIC database. (ED427897)

Article from a Printed Magazine, Reproduced Online

Goetzman, K. (2011, November). Mongolians team up to
preserve huge, grassy commons. *Utne.* Retrieved from
http://www.utne.com/Wild-Green/Mongolians-Team-Up-
to-Preserve-Huge-Grassy-Commons.aspx

Article from an Online Magazine, No Author Listed

How a psychologist can help you control anger. (2010).
APA Online. Retrieved from http://www.apa.org/topics
/anger/help.aspx

Note: Avoid listing page numbers for online articles.

Article from an Online Newspaper

Stein, P. (2011, November 3). Lessons from the garden.
Miami Herald. Retrieved from http://www.miamiherald
.com/2011/11/01/2485264/lessons-from-the-garden.html

Document from University Program or Department

Spence, S. (2012). *Department of language and literature
writing guidelines.* Retrieved from Clayton College
and State University, Department of Humanities
website: http://a-s.clayton.edu/Langlit/guidelines/
default.html

Government Document

U.S. Cong. House. (2011, September 22). *Fairness for
high-skilled immigrants act.* House Resolution 3012.
Retrieved from http://thomas.loc.gov/cgi-bin
/query/z?c112:H.R.3012:

Documents from Discussion Groups or Forums

Smith, M. (2011, November). Green (Living) Review [Archives]. Environmental Discussion Group. Retrieved from http://greenreview.blogspot.com/2011/11/being-frugal-is-not-about-being-mean.html

Newsgroup, Message

Clease, G. V. (2012, April 12). Narrative bibliography [Msg. 41]. Message posted to jymacmillan@mail.csu.edu

11f Formatting a Paper in the APA Style

Compose your research project in the following order:

1. Title page
2. Abstract
3. Introduction, Body, Conclusion
4. References
5. Appendix

Title Page

In addition to your paper's title and your name and academic affiliation, the title page should establish your running head that will appear on every page preceding the page number. See page 167 for an example of a title page in APA style.

Abstract

You should provide an abstract with every paper written in APA style. An abstract is a quick but thorough summary of the contents of your paper. It is read first and may be the only part read, so it must be accurate, self-contained, concise, nonevaluative, and coherent. See page 168 for an example.

Text of the Paper

Double-space your entire paper. In general you *should* use subtitles as side heads and centered heads in your paper. Follow your instructor's guidelines for formatting your paper (e.g., margins, indentions, and use of fonts).

References

Prepare your list of references according to the designs shown in Section 11e, pages 173–174. It should include all sources that are available to others. Do not list personal correspondence or e-mail.

Appendix

The appendix is the appropriate place for material that is not germane to your text but nevertheless has pertinence to the study. Here you can present graphs, charts, study plans, observation and test results, and other matter that will help your reader understand the nature of your work.

11g Sample Paper in APA Style

The following paper demonstrates the format and style of a paper written to the standards of APA style. The paper requires a title page that establishes the running head, an abstract, in-text citations to name and year of each source used, and a list of references. Marginal notations explain specific requirements.

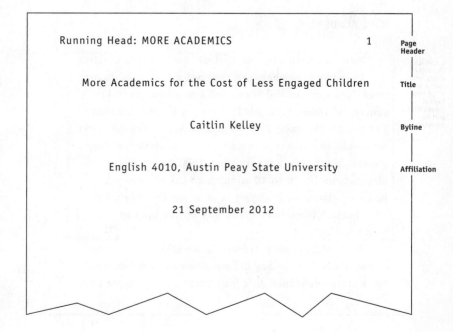

Running Head: MORE ACADEMICS   1   Page
                                                                            Header

More Academics for the Cost of Less Engaged Children   Title

Caitlin Kelley   Byline

English 4010, Austin Peay State University   Affiliation

21 September 2012

MORE ACADEMICS   2

**An abstract
is usually
required for
scientific
writing.**

Abstract

The elimination of elementary school recess periods
was investigated to examine the theoretical implications
of depriving learners of these important mental and
physical stimuli. The goal was to determine the effect of
the modern trend to use recess time for longer academic
periods. The social and psychological implications were
determined by an examination of the literature, including
comments from educational leaders. Results are mixed, as
the end result of an increased emphasis on standardized
testing will not be realized for several years. The social
implications affect the mental and physical lives of school-
aged children who are learning less about cooperation with
their peers and more about remaining stagnant with little
activity for lengthy periods of time.

MORE ACADEMICS   3

**Establish
the topic
along with
social and/
or psycho-
logical
issues that
will be
examined.**

More Academics for the Cost of Less Engaged Children
Everyone remembers the days out on the playground
when "you got skinned knees and bruises and sand in
your eyes" (DeGregory, 2005). Growing up in the 1990s
I remember the days when classes walked to the cafeteria
for lunch, and students could sit next to whomever they
wanted. When they were finished, they were free to
play outside for 30 to 40 minutes on the playground.
However, times are changing, and so are the rules. Not
all school children have the luxury of free play on the
hard top.

In Pinellas County, Florida, in an elementary school
of 800 students, one boy did not know what recess was.
For a class newspaper, this first grade student wrote that

MORE ACADEMICS   4

his favorite day to have gym class was Friday because
the children were allowed "Open Court" because they
were allowed to play whatever they wanted without the
instruction of the teacher. Lane DeGregory (2005), the
journalist who wrote the article, mentioned, "It sounds
just like recess. He's 7 years old and he doesn't know
what recess is." Because this elementary school does
not have recess, the children in Pinellas County only have
25 minutes every Friday to play with one another, explore
and make their own rules to games. However, this school
is not alone; according to Education World, "40 percent
of schools in the United States have cut recess or are
considering dropping it" (Poynter, 2008).

> The theoretical study depends heavily on the literature, which must be cited correctly in APA form.

The question is why are nearly half of the elementary
schools around the country dropping free play and
expression from the daily lives of young children? The
two prevailing reasons are that eliminating free play
reduces the risk of accidents and by eliminating recess,
students have more time in their day for academics, mostly
reading and math (Svensen, 2008). Contradicting these
arguments are mostly parents and doctors who feel that
"recess provides children with the opportunity to develop
friendships, negotiate relationships and build positive
connections" (DeGregory, 2005). The elimination and
reduction of recess in elementary schools to allow more
time for academics is detrimental to the student's mental
and physical well-being.

So who is to say what is best for the children? The
process of eliminating or limiting recess is the decision
of the principal of the elementary school. According to
Greg Toppo (2007, p. 1-A), "the principal of each school
respectively decides whether his or her children need that
extra time for play, or whether it would be better spent on
academics."

> Posing a question in the paper helps to re-emphasize the thesis.

MORE ACADEMICS   5

Use present tense verbs (*takes, proves*) for what happens or can happen now.

    According to Patti Caplan, spokeswoman for the Howard County schools in Washington, DC, principals stated, "Shortening recess by five minutes daily provides 25 minutes of additional instruction time each week" (Matthews, 2004, p. B1). Most schools take their students straight from lunch back to the classroom and start a lecture right away. This lack of a break often proves to be a problem because the students are restless and fidgety (Adelman & Taylor, 2008). In some schools, however, "with the principal's permission, a teacher can take his or her class outside for 15 minutes. For the kids, it's like a jailbreak" (DeGregory, 2005). In the typical classroom, children sit in their seats for up to six hours each day. With academics and curriculum becoming harder, schools need those extra twenty-five minutes each day to teach students everything they will need to know in preparation for the ever-increasing glut of standardized tests. Schools are completely focused on academics, not only so that the students pass the standardized tests, but because "the federal government expects schools to have all children testing at the proficient level in science, language arts and math by the year 2014" (Nussbaum, 2006, p. C1). Unfortunately, these expectations are unable to be reached because of the bell curve; an average will be formulated by the low and high scores, illuminating the possibility of a perfect score. Specifically, not every student can learn and comprehend information in the same way. With the pressure of standardized tests and a more challenging curriculum, "Parents worry about the strain on their children" (Matthews, 2004, p. B1). For this reason, recess for children is even more important than ever. Ginny Mahlke, the principal of Wolftrap Elementary School in Fairfax, Virginia, summed up the shift in a more stringent, performance-based curriculum:

Use the present perfect tense (*will be formulated*) for actions completed and for actions continued into the present time.

MORE ACADEMICS   6

> The increased demands on schools means it is
> even more important now for students to get
> outside, relax, and get some exercise, for every
> minute spent at school is instructional time,
> right down to learning the skills of negotiating
> by deciding whose turn it is on the swing
> (Matthews, 2004, p. B1).

Indent block quotations 1 full tab.

Sharing the opinion of Mahlke are 60% of principals who believe that their students do not learn well without a break because they are fidgety and cannot pay attention sitting in a chair for 6 hours at a time (Adelman & Taylor, 2008). Before the limitations of recess started in the 1980s, students enjoyed breaks for 10 to 20 minutes at a time in the morning, after lunch, and in the afternoon (Nussbaum, 2006, p. C1). In order to give students the recess and the healthy break they need in the middle of the day, some parents argue that if the school days were longer, there would be enough time for a recess break and enough time for the teaching required for the year. Then teachers would not be "forced to choose between recess and instruction. Children need both" (Dulman & Sigall, 2006, p. A22).

The problems with eliminating recess do not just stop on an academic level. Cutting out play time for young children affects their social skills and their physical skills. Students need to learn to make up their own rules and play their own games. With recess, students can experience uninstructed play in contrast to being constantly directed all day (Widhalm, 2004, p. B1). On the playground, with adults serving only as supervisors, children learn to work through altercations, to make decisions, and also how to make friends. It is essential to have physical contact with other children in a world of technology where students often play

MORE ACADEMICS   7

with themselves. Scientists say that "children who
are glued to their computers interact less with other
children, become passive learners, and read less"
(Devi, 2006).

Recess is a physical activity for most children,
which is constructive toward their health and well being.
"Research shows that between more schools eliminating
recess and after-school programs . . . the amount of
time kids spend being physically active is dwindling
significantly" (Tracey, 2005). When children are taken
outside for recess after lunch, they are exposed to and
become used to playing outdoors, an activity that can
be repeated in the home environment. Because of the
stagnant environment of school, too many children would
rather play inside with electronics than go outside. Even
worse than children not getting the exercise they need is
that schools are contributing to childhood obesity. Results
from recent research revealed that "36% of schools sell
treats such as chips, candy and ice cream in the school
cafeteria" (Toppo, 2007, p. 1-A). If children had recess as
an outlet to run around and play, the rates of childhood
obesity would be cut because the children would be
burning calories.

Use the past tense (*outlawed, banned*) to express actions that occurred at a specific time in the past.

The other speculation as to why recess is being
eliminated in schools is that children are being injured
and schools are being sued by parents because of the
injuries ("Tag—you're illegal!" 2006). This reason brings
up the debate of whether or not children are being
nurtured too much and whether they are being made
into weaker human beings because of it. "An elementary
school in Massachusetts that banned tag, dodge ball
and all other 'contact' or 'chase' games" ("Tag—you're
illegal!" 2006) has joined the bandwagon with many
other schools that worry about the scratches and scrapes
of its young children. Another town even "outlawed

MORE ACADEMICS   8

touching altogether" ("Tag—you're illegal!" 2006). It is no wonder why childhood obesity is such a prevalent issue in American society today. Children are not given the opportunity to exercise and have fun, even when they are allowed onto the playground.

Amazingly, only 60% of the nation's elementary schools still have a full 20 to 40 minute recess period after lunch (Poynter, 2008). Students in the 40% of elementary schools who are neglecting the benefits and needs of recess are suffering from it. Children need recess to exercise their bodies and their minds, especially at such a young age when they are still growing and developing. Principals have reasons to back up their decisions for doing away with recess; however, there is more evidence that proves students need the time and exercise that a recess period provides. How will the elimination of recess affect that 40% of children in the United States who do not have play time during the day? Will it stunt their mental growth and become detrimental in the long run? At the present time it is too early to tell because these eliminations are so new; however, the more important question is whether elementary school children today can reach their full potential after being deprived of the mental and physical stimuli that can be experienced on the playground.

The conclusion can include a statement on the state of research in the area of study as well as questions for further research.

References

References begin on a new page.

Adelman, H., & Taylor, L. (2008). Attention problems: Intervention and resources. UCLA Center for Mental Health in Schools. Retrieved from http://smhp.psych .ucla.edu/pdfdocs/Attention/attention.pdf

Citation for an online article from a research center at an institution.

DeGregory, L. (2005, March 29). Boulevard of dreams.
St. Petersburg Times. Retrieved from http://www
.sptimes.com/2005/03/29/Floridian/Out_of_play.shtml

Devi, C. (2006, September 14). When starting them young
is not all. Retrieved from http://www.redorbit.com
/news/technology/655999/when_starting_them_
young_is_not_all/index.html?source=r_technology

Dulman, P. P., & Sigall, B. T. (2006, June 8). Find time for
learning and play. _Washington Post_, p. A22.

Matthews, J. (2004, April 9). Federal education law
squeezes out recess. _Washington Post_, p. B1.

Nussbaum, D. (2006, December 10). Before children ask,
what's recess? _New York Times_, p. C1.

Poynter, A. (2008). The end of recess. Retrieved from
http://www.poynter.org/column.asp?id=2&aid=80426

Svensen, A. (2008). Banning school recess. Retrieved
from http://school.familyeducation.com/educational-
innovation/growth-and-development/38674.html

Tag—you're illegal! (2006, October 28). _Los Angeles
Times_. Retrieved from http://www.latimes.
com/news/opinion/la-ed-tag28oct28,0,59791.
story?coll=la-opinion-leftrail

Toppo, G. (2007, May 16). School recess isn't exactly on
the run. _USA Today_, p. 1-A. Retrieved from EBSCOhost
database.

Tracy, K. (2005, October 6). The fruit fixation. _Variety_.
Retrieved from http://www.variety.com/article
/VR1117930289.html?categoryid=2075&cs=1

Widhalm, S. (2004, March 15). Sometimes you want a
break: Benefits of recess outweigh lost class time,
advocates say. _Washington Post_, p. B1.

Citation for
a newspaper
article.

An Internet
source requires
the words
"Retrieved
from" preceding
the URL.

Citation for an
article from
a library's
database.

12

The Footnote System: CMS Style

Clear Targets

The fine arts and some fields in the humanities, but not literature, use traditional footnotes. This documentation style should conform to standards set by *The Chicago Manual of Style* (CMS), 16th ed., 2010. The following components discussed in this chapter will help to document the references used in your research paper:

- Blending sources into your writing
- Formatting and writing footnotes
- Writing endnotes rather than footnotes
- Writing a bibliography page for a CMS-style research paper

In the CMS system, you must place superscript numerals within the text (like this[15]) and place documentary footnotes on corresponding pages. The discussion in this chapter assumes that notes will appear as footnotes, but some instructors accept endnotes; that is, all notes appear together at the end of the paper, not at the bottom of individual pages. See Section 12e, "Writing Endnotes Rather Than Footnotes."

12a Blending Sources into Your Writing

There are two types of footnotes: the documentary note identifies your sources with bibliographic information; and the other, called a content note, can discuss related matters, explain your methods of research, suggest related literature, provide biographical information, or offer other information that is not immediately pertinent to your discussion. Both types are discussed at length in this chapter.

Introducing the Sources

The first example below implies a source that will be found in the footnote; the second expresses the name in the text. With footnotes, the implied reference is acceptable. With endnotes, however, you should probably use the expressed reference.

Implied reference:

> The organic basis of autism is generally agreed upon. Three possible causes for autism have been identified: behavioral syndrome, organic brain disorder, or a range of biological and psycho social factors.[9]

Expressed reference:

> Martin Rutter has acknowledged that the organic basis of autism is generally agreed upon. Rutter named three possible causes for autism: behavioral syndrome, organic brain disorder, or a range of biological and psychosocial factors.[10]

Inserting a Superscript Numeral in Your Text

Place Arabic numerals typed slightly above the line (like this[12]) with the superscript feature of your word processor. Place a superscript numeral immediately at the end of each quotation or paraphrase, without a space after the final word or mark of punctuation, as in this sample:

> Steven A. LeBlanc, an archaeologist at Harvard University, along with several other scholars, argues instead that "humans have been at each others' throats since the dawn of the species."[1] Arthur Ferrill observes, "When man first learned how to write, he already had war to write about."[2] Ferrill adds, "In prehistoric times man was a hunter and a killer of other men. The killer instinct in the prehistoric male is clearly attested by archaeology in fortifications, weapons, cave paintings, and skeletal remains."[3]

The footnotes that relate to these in-text superscript numerals will appear at the bottom of the page, as shown here:

> 1. See Steven A. LeBlanc, *Constant Battles: The Myth of the Peaceful, Noble Savage* (New York: St. Martin's Press, 2004), 15, and also L. D. Cooper, *Rousseau, Nature, and the Problem of the Good Life* (University Park: Pennsylvania State Univ. Press, 2000).

    2. Arthur Ferrill, "Neolithic Warfare." Accessed 6 April
2011. http://eserver.org/history/neolithic-war.txt.
    3. Ibid.

For a subsequent reference to an immediately preceding source, use "Ibid." in roman typeface (not in italics and not underscored).

Writing Full or Abbreviated Notes

CMS style permits you to omit a bibliography page as long as you give full bibliographic details in each source's initial footnote.

    1. Nouriel Roubini and Stephen Mihm, *Crisis Economics: A Crash Course in the Future of Finance* (New York: Penguin, 2011), 49.

However, you may provide a comprehensive bibliography to each source and abbreviate all footnotes, even the initial ones, since full data will be found in the bibliography.

    1. Roubini and Mihm, *Crisis Economics: A Crash Course in the Future of Finance*, 49.

The bibliography entry would read this way:

Roubini, Nouriel, and Stephen Mihm. *Crisis Economics: A Crash Course in the Future of Finance*. New York: Penguin, 2011.

12b Formatting and Writing the Footnotes

Place a footnote on the same page as its corresponding text reference. Endnotes, however, appear all together at the end of your paper in a "Notes" section. Single-space footnote text, but double-space between the notes. For endnotes, double-space as in the body of your paper. Indent the first line of each footnote or endnote five spaces.

Number the notes consecutively through the entire paper. Use a raised superscript numeral for the in-text citation. Use a normal number next to the text of the note.

Separate footnotes from the text by triple spacing or, if you prefer, by a line extending 12 spaces from the left margin. See the sample paper, pages 184–190.

Book

List the author, followed by a comma, the title underlined or in the italics font, the publication data within parentheses (city: publisher, year), followed by a comma and the page number(s). Unless ambiguity would result, the abbreviations *p.* and *pp.* may be omitted.

1. Robert Norman Rapoport, *Children, Youth, and Families: The Action-Research Relationship* (New York: Cambridge Univ. Press, 2011), 20–23.

List two authors without a comma:

2. Marc Vachon and Amy Vachon, *Equally Shared Parenting: Rewriting the Rules for a New Generation of Parents* (New York: Penguin, 2011), 18.

Note: Publisher's names are spelled out in full but the words *Company* or *Inc.* are omitted. Reference to an edition follows the title or the editors, if listed (see footnote 3).

For more than three authors, use *et al.* after mention of the lead author:

3. Andrew C. Garrod et al., eds., "Introduction," *Adolescent Portraits: Identity, Relationships, and Challenges*, 7th ed. (Boston: Allyn & Bacon, 2011), 3.

For a subsequent reference to an immediately preceding source, use "Ibid." in the roman typeface, not in italics and not underscored:

4. Ibid.

Journal Article

5. Vladimir M. Sloutsky and Anna V. Fisher, "Linguistic Labels: Conceptual Markers or Object Features," *Journal of Experimental Child Psychology* 111 (2011): 65–86.

Magazine Article

6. Angus Maclachlan, "Guess Who Came to Dinner," *Smithsonian*, November 2011, 108.

Newspaper Article

7. John Kirkenfeld, "Digging for More Dirt," *Mill City Daily News*, 23 July 2011, 1A.

Nonprint Source: Lecture, Sermon, Speech, Oral Report

8. Dick Weber, "The Facts About Preparing Teens to Drive" (lecture, Dutchtown High School, Locust Grove, GA, October 16, 2011).

Encyclopedia

9. *The World Book Encyclopedia*, 2010 ed., s.v. "Raphael."

Note: "s.v." means *sub verbo*, "under the word(s)."

Government Documents

10. United States. Dept. of the Treasury, "Financial Operations of Government Agencies and Funds," *Treasury Bulletin*, Washington, DC, June 2010, 134–141.

11. U.S., *Constitution*, art. 1, sec. 4.

12. United Kingdom, *Coroner's Act, 1954*, 2 & 3 Eliz. 2, ch.31.

Television

13. Bob Schieffer, *CBS News*, February 13, 2012.

Film on DVD

14. *Breakfast at Tiffany's*, DVD, directed by Blake Edwards (Hollywood, CA: Paramount, 1961).

Biblical Reference

15. Matt. 10:5.

16. 1 Pet. 5:1–4 (New Revised Standard Edition).

12c Writing Footnotes for Electronic Sources

To cite electronic sources, *The Chicago Manual of Style* includes a publication date, date of access, and the URL. The models here show these requirements.

Article Online

17. Arthur Ferril, "Neolithic Warfare" Frontline Educational Foundation, accessed February 19, 2012, http://eserver.org/history/neolithic-war.txt.

Magazine Article Reproduced Online

18. James Owens, "Baby Mammoth CT Scan Reveals Internal Organs," *National Geographic News*, 11 April 2008, accessed January 27, 2012, http://news.nationalgeographic.com/news/2008/04/080411-baby-mammoth.html.

Journal Article Reproduced Online

19. Kimberly A. Tyler and Katherine A. Johnson, "Exemplifying the Integrations of the Relational Developmental System: Synthesizing Theory, Research, and Application to Promote Positive Development and Social Justice," *Journal of Adolescent Research* 23 (2008): 245–55, accessed November 7, 2011, http://jar.sagepub.com/cgi/reprint/23/3/245.

Article from a Database

20. NASA/IPAC Extragalactic Database, http://nedwww. ipac.caltech.edu/ (object name IRAS F004000+4059; accessed March 13, 2011).

Article Accessed from a Database Through the Library System

21. Victor Davis Hanson, "War Will Be War: No Matter the Era, No Matter the Weapons, and the Same Old Hell." *National Review,* 54 (2002), accessed January 27, 2011, available from InfoTrac database, Art. A84943306.

Book Online

22. Sarah Morgan Dawson, *A Confederate Girl's Diary*, 1913, (Univ. of Maryland, 2011), accessed April 3, 2011, http:// docsouth.unc.edu/fpn/dawson/menu.html.

CD-ROM Source

23. The Old Testament, *The Bible,* Bureau Development, CD-ROM.

Article from an Online Service

24. Jennifer Viegas, "Genocide Wiped Out Native American Population," *Discovery News*, September 26, 2010, accessed September 29, 2010, http://news.discovery.com/archaeology/ genocide-native-americans-ethnic-cleansing.html.

E-mail

Because e-mail is not retrievable, do not document with a footnote or bibliography entry. Instead, mention the nature of the source within your text by saying something like this:

Walter Wallace argues that teen violence stems mainly from the breakup of the traditional family (e-mail to the author).

12d Writing Subsequent Footnote References

After a first full footnote, references to the same source should be shortened to the author's last name and page number. When an author has two works mentioned, employ a shortened version of the title, "3. Jones, *Paine*, 25." In general, avoid Latinate abbreviations such as *loc. cit.* or *op. cit.*; however, whenever a note refers to the source in the immediately preceding note, you may use "Ibid." alone or "Ibid." with a page number, as shown below. If the subsequent note does not refer to the one immediately above it, do not use "Ibid." Instead, repeat the author's last name (note especially the difference between notes 2 and 4):

1. Robert E. Slavin, *Educational Psychology: Theory and Practice*, 10th ed. (New York: Prentice Hall, 2011), 23.
2. Ibid., 27.
3. Grant P. Wiggins and Jay McTighe, *Understanding by Design*, 2nd ed. (Alexandria, VA: ASCD, 2005), 91.
4. Slavin, 24.
5. Ibid., 27.

Note: Single-space footnotes but double-space between each note.

12e Writing Endnotes Rather than Footnotes

With permission of your instructor, put all your notes together as a single group of endnotes to lessen the burden of typing the paper. Most word-processing programs allow users to insert superscript numerals referencing sources in text and then type the endnotes consecutively at the end of the text, not at the bottom of each page. The list should be titled "Notes" and should be double-spaced throughout. Conform to the following example:

Notes

1. Christine Carter, *Raising Happiness: 10 Simple Steps for More Joyful Kids and Happier Parents* (New York: Random House, 2010), 24.
2. Ibid., 27.
3. Ellen Galinsky, *Mind in the Making: The Seven Essential Life Skills Every Child Needs—Breakthrough Research Every Parent Should Know* (New York: HarperCollins, 2010), 221.
4. Michele Borba, "10 Tips for Raising Moral Kids," accessed June 17, 2011, http://www.micheleborba.com/Pages/ArtBMI13.htm.

5. Carter, 28.

6. Marc Vachon and Amy Vachon, *Equally Shared Parenting: Rewriting the Rules for a New Generation of Parents* (New York: Farrar, Straus, and Young, 2008), 113.

7. Ibid., 114.

8. Borba.

9. Carter, 28.

12f Writing Content Footnotes or Content Endnotes

As a general rule, put important matters in your text. Use a content note to explain research problems, conflicts in the testimony of the experts, matters of importance that are not germane to your discussion, interesting tidbits, credit to people and sources not mentioned in the text, and other matters that might interest readers. The following samples demonstrate two types of content endnotes.

Related Matters Not Germane to the Text

1. The problems of politically correct language are explored in Adams, Tucker (4–5), Zalers, and also Young and Smith (583). These authorities cite the need for caution by administrators who would impose new measures on speech and behavior. Verbal abuse cannot be erased by a new set of unjust laws. Patrick German offers several guidelines for implementing an effective but reasonable program (170–72).

Literature on a Related Topic

2. For additional study of the effects of alcoholics on children, see especially the *Journal of Studies on Alcohol* for the article by Wolin et al. and the bibliography on the topic by Orme and Rimmer (285–87). In addition, group therapy for children of alcoholics is examined in Hawley and Brown.

12g Writing a Bibliography Page for a Paper That Uses Footnotes

If you write completely documented footnotes, the bibliography is redundant. Check with your instructor before preparing one because it may not be required. Separate the title from the first entry with a triple-space. Type the first line of each entry flush left; indent the second line and other succeeding lines five spaces or one-half inch.

Alphabetize the list by last names of authors. Double-space the entries as shown below. List alphabetically by title two or more works by one author. The basic forms are as follows:

Book

Haslam, Jonathan. *Russia's Cold War: From the October Revolution to the Fall of the Wall.* New Haven, CT: Yale Univ. Press, 2011.

Journal Article

Gerlach, Jeanne Marcum. "An Extraordinary Century for Women." *English Journal* 101 (September 2011): 69–75.

Newspaper

Osher, Christopher N. "Tax Break Blurs Lines." *Denver Post* 7 November 2011, 1A+.

Internet Article

"Biography." Paul Laurence Dunbar Website. Accessed February 23, 2012. http://www.dunbarsite.org/biopld.asp.

If the author is known, provide the date when the page was "last modified."

Kaufman, Rachel. "New Species Found: Thai Fossils Reveal Ancient Primate." *National Geographic News.* Last modified March 11, 2011. http://www.nationalgeographic.com/news/2011/03110311-new-species-found-fossils-primates-tarsiers-thailand-science/.

12h Sample Research Paper in CMS Style

The essay that follows demonstrates the format and documentation style that you should use for a research paper when the instructor asks that you use "footnotes," the Chicago style, or the CMS style, all of which refer to *The Chicago Manual of Style.* If permitted, notes may be placed at the end of the paper as double spaced endnotes rather than at the bottom of the pages.

Note: A title page is required only when you have an outline or other prefatory material. If a professor requires a title page and outline, consult page 167 for a sample title page and pages 87–89 for information on writing an outline.

Johnston 1

Name and course information precede the title. No separate title page is necessary unless you provide an outline, abstract, or other prefatory matter.

Jamie Johnston

English Composition 1020

11 April 2012

   Prehistoric Wars: We've Always Hated Each Other

   Here we are, a civilized world with reasonably

educated people, yet we constantly fight with other. These

are not sibling squabbles either; people die in terrible

ways. We wonder, then, if there was ever a time when

men and women lived in harmony with one another and

with nature and the environment. The Bible speaks of the

Garden of Eden, and the French philosopher Jean-Jacques

Rousseau advanced the idea in the 1700s of the "noble

savage," and that "nothing could be more gentle" than an

ancient colony of people.[1] Wrong!

The writer uses the introduction to discuss historical evidence.

   Steven A. LeBlanc, an archaeologist at Harvard

University, along with several other scholars, argues

instead that "humans have been at each others' throats

since the dawn of the species."[2] Robin Yates, for example,

says the ancient ancestors of the Chinese used "long-range

projectile weapons" as long ago as 28,000 BC for both

hunting and "intrahuman conflict."[3] Arthur Ferrill observes,

"When man first learned how to write, he already had war

---

   [1]See Steven A. LeBlanc, *Constant Battles: The Myth of the Peaceful, Noble Savage* (New York: St. Martin's Press, 2004), 15, and also L. D. Cooper, *Rousseau, Nature, and the Problem of the Good Life* (University Park: Pennsylvania State Univ. Press, 2000).

Citation for a magazine

   [2]Steven A. LeBlanc, "Prehistory of Warfare," *Archaeology* (May/June, 2003), 18.

   [3]Robin Yates, "Early China," in *War and Society in the Ancient and Medieval Worlds*, ed. Kurt Raaflaub and Nathan Rosenstein (Cambridge, MA: Center for Hellenic Studies, 2001): 9.

Citation for a book

Johnston 2

to write about."[4] Ferrill adds, "In prehistoric times man was a hunter and a killer of other men. The killer instinct in the prehistoric male is clearly attested by archaeology in fortifications, weapons, cave paintings, and skeletal remains."[5]

Evidence proves that savage fighting occurred in the ancient history of human beings. We have evidence of the types of weapons employed. We can also list reasons for the prehistoric fighting. This paper will examine those items, but the crux of the debate centers on the inducement or instinct. Were early humans motivated by biological instincts or by cultural demands for a share of limited resources? That's the issue this paper will address.

This section opens with the writer's thesis to introduce the issue.

First, we need to look briefly at the evidence. Kelly Hearn has reported on the work of one forensic archaeologist, Christina Conlee, who has investigated a rare headless skeleton with a "ceramic head jar" in the Nasca region of southern Peru.[6] The victim "was killed in a rite of ancestral worship. This information provides new information on human sacrifice in the ancient Andes and in particular on decapitation and trophy heads."[7] Conlee has the proof of the executions, but not the reason, although speculations center on religious ceremonies. Anthropologists continue to study the "head jar" which is "painted with two inverted human faces."[8] Other

---

[4]Arthur Ferrill, "Neolithic Warfare" Frontline Educational Foundation, accessed April 6, 2012, http://eserver.org/history/neolithic-war.txt.

Citation for an Internet source

[5]Ibid.

[6]Kelly Hearn, "Decapitated Man Found in Peru Tomb with Ceramic 'Replacement' Head" *National Geographic News*, 6 June 2007, accessed April 5, 2012, http://news.nationalgeographic.com/news/2007/06/070606-head-jar.html.

The word *Ibid* refers to the immediately preceding note.

[7]Ibid.

[8]Ibid.

Johnston 3

researchers suggest that the victims were prisoners of war and not the losers of ritual combat. In either case, the ancients were less than noble savages.

LeBlanc's book *Constant Battles* is a catalog of prehistoric fighting, David Webster describes the savage fighting of the ancient Mayans,[9] and Nick Thorpe in *British Archaeology* describes massacres that occurred in Europe over 8,500 years ago—decapitation, scalping, axe blows, and other nasty methods.[10] Indeed, articles are now available on wars in ancient Japan, Egypt, Greece,[11] and the Southwestern areas of the United States.[12]

The weapons, too, have been uncovered: clubs, arrowheads, bows, slings, daggers, maces, and spears. Each weapon graduated upon the previous and served new purposes as armies gathered for combat. One source points out that "the bow and the sling were important for hunting, but the dagger and mace were most useful for fighting other humans."[13] The spear required close combat. The bow and arrow had a range of about 100 yards. The sling was a significant weapon because in the right hands it was accurate from long distances and very powerful with stones that could crush skulls.

---

[9]David Webster, "Ancient Maya Warfare," in *War and Society in the Ancient and Medieval Worlds*, ed. Kurt Raaflaub and Nathan Rosenstein (Cambridge, MA: Center for Hellenic Studies, 2001), 333–60.

[10]Nick Thorpe, "Origins of War: Mesolithic Conflict in Europe," *British Archaeology* 52 (2000), accessed April 7, 2012, http://www.birtarch.ac.uk/ba/ba52/ba52feat.html.

[11]See Kurt Raaflaub and Nathan Rosenstein.

[12]See LeBlanc, "Prehistory of Warfare" and also *Constant Battles*.

[13]"Prehistoric Warfare," accessed April 7, 2012, http://digilander.libero.it/tepec/prehistoric_warfare.htm.

For spacing considerations, a portion of this research paper has been omitted.

Johnston 7

Yet, in my opinion (I have to reach my own conclusion here), the biological history of men and women suggests that we love a good fight. I recall reading an article that said twins inside the womb actually fight, and one fetus might actually devour or absorb the other one. Sibling just naturally fight, as I did with my older sister and younger brother. His anger exploded one time, and he broke my arm by hitting me with a shovel. We all have witnessed the terrible fights at sporting events, and recently at Glenbrook North High School in Northbrook, Illinois, hazing turned into a terrible beating for some girls. Oh sure, we can give reasons for our eagerness to fight—to preserve our honor ("Don't diss me!), to preserve our freedom ("Don't encroach!"), or because of fear ("Don't hit me 'cause I'll be hitting back even harder!"). Yet in a final analysis, people want power over others—men beat their wives, mothers overly spank their children, the better team overpowers an opponent, and, yes, a larger, stronger nation will demolish another if self-interest prevails.

This is human nature. The men of Al Quida who flew their suicide missions into the World Trade Center and the Pentagon knew exactly what they were doing—exercising their power. In effect, they said, "We'll show the United States that we can inflict great damage." Professor Donald Kagan observes:

> In the end what people really go to war about is power, by which I simply mean the ability to have their will prevail. . . . Every being and every nation requires power for two purposes. The first is to be

The writer's conclusion connects his thesis to the modern emphasis on war and terrorism.

---

[23]Hanson, ibid.

[24]Jones, Peter. "Ancient and Modern," *Spectator* 291 (2003), accessed April 7, 2012, http://spectator.co.uk/columnists/all/767441/ancient-and-modern.html.

Johnston 8

able to do what it wishes to and must do, some of
which will be good and perfectly natural things.
Second, one needs power to keep others from
imposing their will, to prevent evil things from
being done.[25]

The sport of boxing continues to thrive, despite
attempts to end it because of its brutality. The fans have
a vicarious thrill as one boxer gets pounded to the canvas.
At NASCAR races the greatest shouts occur as the fenders
crash and cars go tumbling topsy-turvy down the asphalt.
The aggressive behavior of humans is not always a pretty
sight, such as the eager willingness of some to loot and
pilfer a neighborhood that has been hit by a tornado or
other natural disaster.

At the same time, a country like ours governs itself,
imposing order by law and moral behavior by religion.[26]
Our government, our culture, and our sense of honor have
prevailed in a world of nations gone berserk and lawless.
Whether we should use our power to impose our sense of
democracy on other countries is an international question
without a clear answer. My brother, with the shovel in his
hand, would say "yes."

---

[25]Kagan.

[26]When chaos develops, as in Baghdad during the
2003 war, lawless looting and violence emerge because
neither the religious leaders nor an absent police force
can maintain order. The breakdown of the culture opens a
vacuum filled quickly by primitive behavior.

Johnston 9

Bibliography

Adams, Michael. "The 'Good War' Myth and the Cult of
Nostagia." *The Midwest Quarterly* 40 (1998). http://
www.accessmylibrary.com/archive/739-the-midwest-
quarterly/september-1998.html.

Cooper, L. D. *Rousseau, Nature, and the Problem of the
Good Life.* University Park: Pennsylvania State Univ
.Press, 2000.

Ferrill, Arthur. "Neolithic Warfare." Frontline Educational
Foundation. http://eserver.org/history/neolithic-war
.txt.

Hanson, Victor Davis. "War Will Be War: No Matter the
Era, No Matter the Weapons, and the Same Old Hell."
National Review 54 (2002). http://goliath.ecnext.com/
coms2/gi_0199-1746598/War-Will-Be-War-No.html

Hearn, Kelly. "Decapitated Man Found in Peru Tomb with
Ceramic 'Replacement' Head." *National Geographic
News.* Last modified 6 June 2007. http://news
.nationalgeographic.com/news/2007/06/070606-head-
jar.html.

Jones, Peter. "Ancient and Modern." *Spectator* 291 (2003).
http://www.spectator.co.uk/columnists/all/767441/
ancient-and-modern.thtml.

Kagan, Donald. "History's Largest Lessons." Interview by
Fredric Smoler. *American Heritage* 48 (1997). http://
www.americanheritage.com/articles/magazine/
ah/1997/1/1997_1_58_print.shtml.

LeBlanc, Steven A. *Constant Battles: The Myth of the
Peaceful, Noble Savage.* New York: St. Martin's Press,
2004.

---. "Prehistory of Warfare." *Archaeology,* May/June, 2003.

Parsell, D. L. "City Occupied by Inca Discovered on Andean
Peak in Peru." *National Geographic News.* Last modified
March 21, 2002. http://news.nationalgeographic
.com/news/2002/03/0314_0318_vilcabamba.html.

A separate
bibliography
page is not
required if you
provide full
bibliographic
details in each
of your initial
footnotes.

Johnston 10

"Prehistoric Warfare. " Last modified March 11, 2011.
http://www.worldlingo.com/ma/enwiki/en/
Prehistoric_warfare.

Shy, John. "The Cultural Approach to the History of War."
The Journal of Military History 57 (1993). http://
people.cohums.ohio-state.edu/grimsley1/Race/shy
.pdf.

Thorpe, Nick. "Origins of War: Mesolithic Conflict in
Europe." *British Archaeology* 52 (2000). http://www
.birtarch.ac.uk/ba/ba52/ba52feat.html.

Webster, David. "Ancient Maya Warfare." In *War and Society
in the Ancient and Medieval Worlds*. Ed. Kurt Raaflaub
and Nathan Rosenstein. Cambridge, MA: Center for
Hellenic Studies, 2001.

Yates, Robin. "Early China." In *War and Society in the
Ancient and Medieval Worlds*. Ed. Kurt Raaflaub and
Nathan Rosenstein. Cambridge, MA: Center for Hellenic
Studies, 2001.

13

CSE Style for the Natural and Applied Sciences

Clear Targets

The Council of Science Editors has established two separate forms for citing sources in scientific writing. One is the **citation-sequence** system for writing in the applied sciences, such as chemistry, computer science, mathematics, physics, and the medicine sciences. This system uses numbers in the text rather than a name and year. The second style format is the **name-year** system for use in the biological and earth sciences. The elements discussed in this chapter will assist with the CSE documentation style for your research paper:

- Writing in-text citations using the citation-sequence system
- Writing a references page
- Formatting a paper in CSE style

The citation-sequence system saves space and the numbers make minimal disruption to the reading of the text, yet this style seldom mentions names, so readers must refer to the bibliography for the names of authors.

Citation-Sequence

The original description (3) contained precise taxonomic detail that differed with recent studies (4–6).

Name-Year

The original description (Roberts 2010) contained precise taxonomic detail that differed with recent studies (McCormick 2012a, 2012b, and Tyson and others 2011).

13a Writing In-Text Citations Using the CSE Citation-Sequence System

Use this citation style with these disciplines: chemistry, computer science, mathematics, physics, and the medical sciences (medicine, nursing, and general health). In simple terms, the style requires an in-text *number*, rather than the year, and a list of "Cited References" that are numbered to correspond to the in-text citations.

After completing a list of references, assign a number to each entry. Use one of two methods for numbering the list: (1) arrange references in alphabetical order and number them consecutively (in which case the numbers appear in random order in the text); or (2) number the references consecutively as you put them into your text, interrupting that order when entering references cited earlier.

The number serves as the key reference to the source, as numbered in the "Cited References." Conform to the following guidelines:

1. Place the number within parentheses (1) or brackets [2] or as a superscript numeral like this ([5]). A name is not required and is even discouraged, so try to arrange your wording accordingly. Full information on the author and the work will be found in the references list.

   It is known [1] that the DNA concentration of a nucleus doubles during interphase.

   A recent study [1] has raised interesting questions related to photosynthesis, some of which have been answered [2].

   In particular, a recent study[1] has raised many interesting questions related to photosynthesis, some of which have been answered.[2]

2. If the sentence uses the authority's name, add the number after the name.

   Additional testing by Cooper (3) includes alterations in carbohydrate metabolism and changes in ascorbic acid incorporation into the cell and adjoining membranes.

3. If necessary, add specific data to the entry:

   "The use of photosynthesis in this application is crucial to the environment" (Skelton,[8] p 732).

   The results of the respiration experiment published by Jones (3, Table 6, p 412) had been predicted earlier by Smith (5, Proposition 8).

13b Writing a Cited References Page

Supply a list of references at the end of your paper. Number it to correspond to sources as you cite them in the text. An alternate method is to alphabetize the list and then number it. Label the list "Cited References." The form of the entries should duplicate the examples shown below.

Book

Provide a number and then list the author, title of the book, place of publication, publisher, year, and total number of pages (optional).

> 1. Goldschneider K. Clinical Pediatric Anesthesia: A Case-Based Handbook. New York: Oxford University; 2012. 784 p.

Article in a Journal

Provide a number and then list the author, the title of the article, the name of the journal, the year and month if necessary, volume number and issue number if necessary, and inclusive pages. The month or an issue number is necessary for any journal that is paged anew with each issue.

> 2. McLean S. Black goo: Forceful encounters with matter in Europe's muddy margins. Cultural Anthropology. 2011; 26:589–619.

Internet Articles and Other Electronic Publications

Add at the end of the citation an availability statement as well as the date you accessed the material.

> 3. Lyness D. Making a change in your life. 2010. Available from http://kidshealth.org/teen/food_fitness/exercise/ make_change.html. Accessed 2012 Mar 8.
>
> 4. Qiao H, May JM. CpG methylation at the USF-binding site mediates cell-specific transcription of human ascorbate transporter SVCT2 exon 1a. Biochem J. [serial online] 2011. Available from http://www.biochemj.org/bj/440/ bj4400073.htm. Accessed 2012 Feb 8.

Magazine and Newspaper Articles

Add a specific date and, for newspapers, cite a section letter or number.

> 5. [Anonymous]. The gift of light. Tennessee Conservationist
>   2011 Nov/Dec:35.
> 6. Paine A. Metro water hopes windmill whips up savings. The
>   [Nashville] Tennessean 2011 Nov 10; Sect B:1.

Proceedings and Conference Presentations

After supplying a number, give the name of the author or editor, the title of the presentation, the name of the conference, the type of work (reports, proceedings, proceedings online, and so on), the name of the organization or society, the date of the conference, and the place. If found on the Internet, add the URL and the date you accessed the information.

> 7. Lurie N, Garza A, Kahn AS, Kamoie, B, Lipkin, WI, Burns,
>   SZ. Fact or fiction: The science behind movie-making
>   and the film. *Contagion* [abstract online]. In: Abstracts:
>   19th National Conference on Chronic Disease Prevention
>   and Control; 2012 Feb 23; Anaheim(CA). Available from
>   http://www.phprep.org/2012/agenda/plenary.cfm.
>   Accessed 2012 Mar 28.

13c Sample Paper Using the CSE Citation-Sequence System

Diabetes Management:
A Delicate Balance

Balance the title, name, and academic affiliation on a title page.

Sarah E. Bemis
English 103: College Writing
Sister Winifred Morgan, O.P.
5 March 2012

Bemis ii

Abstract

Diabetes affects approximately 11 million people in the U.S. alone, leading to $350 billion in medical costs. Two types, I and II, have debilitating effects. The body may tolerate hyperglycemia for a short time, but severe complications can occur, such as arterioscleroses, heart disease, nerve damage, and cerebral diseases. New drugs continue to improve the lifestyle of a person with diabetes, but controlling blood sugar requires three elements working together—medication, diet, and exercise. This study examines the importance of each of the three. Patients need a controlled balance of the medication, diet, and exercise program.

An abstract of 100–200 words states the purpose, scope, and major findings of the study.

In CSE style, the Abstract is placed on a separate page with Roman numbering.

Bemis 1

Diabetes Management:
A Delicate Balance

Diabetes is a disease that affects approximately 11 million people in the U.S. alone (1), and its complications lead to hundreds of thousands of deaths per year and cost the nation billions in medical care for the direct cost of complications and for indirect costs of lost productivity related to the disease. The condition can produce devastating side effects and a multitude of chronic health problems. For this reason, it can be very frightening to those who do not understand the nature and treatment of the disease. Diabetes currently has no known cure, but it can be controlled. Diabetes research has made great advancements in recent years, but the most important insights into the management of this disease are those which seem the most simplistic. By

Use a number to reference the use of a source.

The thesis or hypothesis is expressed usually at the end of the introduction.

Bemis 2

instituting a healthy, balanced lifestyle, most persons with diabetes can live free of negative side effects.

Scientific writing requires precise definition.

Diabetes mellitus, according to several descriptions, is a disorder in which the body cannot properly metabolize glucose or sugar. The body's inability to produce or properly use insulin permits glucose to build up in the bloodstream. The excess sugar in the blood,

More than one source can be listed for one idea or concept.

or hyperglycemia, is what leads to the side effects of diabetes (2,3,4).

There are actually two types of diabetes. Type I, or juvenile diabetes, is the name given to the condition in which the pancreas produces very little or no insulin. It is normally discovered during childhood, but can occur at any age (3). Adult onset, or type II diabetes, occurs when the pancreas produces usable insulin, but not enough to counteract the amount of glucose in the blood. This often results from obesity or poor diet.

Causal analysis, as shown here, is a staple of scientific writing.

In both type I and type II diabetes, the problem has been identified as hyperglycemia (5). This buildup of glucose in the bloodstream leads to a number of dangerous side effects. The initial effects and indicators of hyperglycemia are frequent urination, intense thirst, increased hunger, and fatigue. When glucose begins to build up in the blood, the kidneys begin to filter out the excess sugar into the urine. The amount of glucose the kidneys can filter varies with each person. In this process, all the water in the body's tissues is being used to produce urine to flush glucose from the kidneys. This is what leads to the intense thirst and frequent urination associated with hyperglycemia (5).

Because the body lacks the insulin needed to allow glucose into the cells, the glucose cannot be processed to produce energy. The cells signal the brain that they are not getting sugar and this causes hunger. However, no matter how much a victim of hyperglycemic diabetes eats, the cells will not be producing energy (6).

Bemis 3

It has been shown (4) that with hyperglycemia the kidneys try to compensate for the excess of sugar and lack of energy. While the kidneys attempt to filter the sugar from the blood, the liver tries to produce energy by burning fat and muscle to produce ketones, a protein that the body attempts to burn in place of glucose. Ketones do not provide the energy the body requires but do produce chemicals toxic to the body. When too many ketones are present in the blood, ketoacidosis occurs (4).

Refer to sources in the past tense or present perfect tense.

Guthrie and Guthrie (1) have demonstrated that ketoacidosis is a condition caused by high levels of hydrogen in the blood. This leads initially to a high blood pH, depleted saline fluids and dehydration. If untreated it can lead to a shutdown of the central nervous system, coma, or even death. In fact, many diabetes-related deaths are caused by ketoacidosis that has reached a comatose state. Ketoacidosis is characterized by frequent urination, dry mouth, extreme thirst, headache, rapid and deep respiration, increased heart rate, nausea, vomiting, disorientation, and lethargy (1).

In addition to a number, you may give the last name of a source.

For spacing considerations, a portion of this research paper has been omitted.

Bemis 7

While it is important to have the proper medication, the backbone of diabetes management is the meal plan. By making wise choices in eating, persons with diabetes can reduce stress on the body and increase the effectiveness of their medication. The basis of a good meal plan is balanced nutrition and moderation. Eating a low-fat, low-sodium, low-sugar diet is the best way for a diabetic to ensure longevity and health. It is important for everyone to eat balanced meals on a routine schedule. For victims of diabetes, it can help in blood sugar control and in preventing heart disease and digestive problems.

The writer explores the second method for controlling diabetes—diet.

Two established meal plans are recommended for patients: the Exchange Plan and carbohydrate counting (12,13). Both are based on the Diabetes Food Pyramid (Nutrition). The Food Pyramid divides food into six groups. These resemble the traditional four food groups, except that they are arranged in a pyramid in which the bottom, or largest, section contains the foods that should be eaten most each day. The top, or smallest, section contains the foods that should be eaten least, if at all. With any diabetic meal plan, the patient should eat a variety of foods from all the food groups, except the sweets, fats, and alcohol group. New directives by the American Diabetes Association offer helpful and authoritative guidance to help victims cope with their meal planning (14,15).

The Exchange Plan provides a very structured meal plan. Foods are divided into eight categories, which are more specific than the groups of the Food Pyramid. A dietician or physician determines a daily calorie range for the patient and, based on that range, decides how many servings she or he should eat from each category per meal. Portion sizes are determined and must be followed exactly. The patient then has the option to either choose foods that fit into the groups recommended for each meal or exchange foods from one group for foods from another.

Bemis 8

Another meal plan patients can utilize is carbohydrate counting. This plan is less structured and gives the patient more flexibility in making meal choices. It also involves less planning. Once again, food is categorized, but into only three groups. The largest food group, carbohydrates, encompasses not only starches but dairy products, fruits, and vegetables as well. The dietician or physician again assigns a calorie range. With this plan, however, only the number of carbohydrates per meal are assigned, and even this is flexible. This plan is recommended for those who know how to make balanced meal choices but need to keep track of their food intake. Once again, portion sizes are important, and the patient must remember to eat the recommended amount of foods from each pyramid category (5,11,12).

The final element in successfully managing diabetes is exercise. It has been shown (16) that exercise can help stimulate the body to use glucose for energy, thus taking it out of the blood. Diabetic patients need regular exercise programs that suit their personal needs. Something as simple as a walking routine can significantly reduce blood glucose levels (16). Some patients may require as little as a fifteen-minute per day walk, where some may need a more involved workout. In each case, an exercise schedule works with meal plans, medication, and lifestyle. Also crucial to the success of an exercise routine is close monitoring of blood sugar. If glucose levels are too high or too low, exercise will have negative effects.

The writer explores the third method for controlling diabetes—exercise.

Bemis 9

All of the aspects of diabetes management can be summed up in one word: balance. Diabetes itself is caused by a lack of balance of insulin and glucose in the body. In order to restore that balance, a person with diabetes must juggle medication, monitoring, diet, and exercise. Managing diabetes is not an easy task, but a long and healthy life is very possible when the delicate balance is carefully maintained.

Bemis 10

References

Cited references follow the same number sequence as in the paper. For details on the year-date system, see pages 155–174.

1. Guthrie DW, Guthrie RA. Nursing management of diabetes mellitus. New York: Springer, 2008. 500 p.

2. [Anonymous]. Diabetes insipidus. American Academy of Family Physicians. Available from http://familydoctor.org/familydoctor/en/diseases-conditions/diabetes-insipidus/symptoms.html. Accessed 2012 Feb 20.

3. Clark CM, Fradkin JE, Hiss RG, Lorenz RA, Vinicor F, Warren-Boulton E. Promoting early diagnosis and treatment of type 2 diabetes. JAMA 2000; 284: 363–365.

4. [Anonymous]. Diabetes: Monitoring your blood sugar level. American Academy of Family Physicians. Available from http://familydoctor.org/familydoctor/en/diseases-conditions/diabetes/treatment/monitoring-your-blood-sugar-level.html. Accessed 2012 Feb 19.

5. Peters AL. Conquering diabetes. New York: Penguin, 2006. 368 p.

Bemis 11

6. Arangat AV, Gerich JE. Type 2 diabetes: postprandial hyperglycemia and increased cardiovascular risk. Vascular Health and Risk Management 2010 Mar; 6:145–155.

7. Milchovich SK, Dunn-Long B. Diabetes mellitus. Boulder, CO: Bull, 2011. 240 p.

8. Davile A. Complications. Diabetes Hands Foundation 2012. Available from http://www.tudiabetes.org/ notes/Complications. Accessed 2012 Feb 21.

9. Hu FB, Li TY, Colditz GA, Willett WC, Manson JE. Television watching and other sedentary behaviors in relation to risk of obesity and type 2 diabetes mellitus in women. JAMA 2003; 289:1785–91.

10. [Anonymous]. Insulin pump therapy. Children with Diabetes 2012. Available from http://www .childrenwithdiabetes.com/pumps/. Accessed 2012 Feb 21.

11. [Anonymous]. Glucophage. Diabetes Healthsource. 2002. Available from http://www.glucophage.com. Accessed 2012 Feb 23.

12. McDermott MT. Endocrine secrets. New York: Elsevier, 2009. 448 p.

13. Bittencourt JA. The power of carbohydrates, proteins, and lipids. Charleston, SC: Createspace, 2011. 196 p.

14. American Diabetes Association. The American Diabetes Association complete guide to diabetes. Alexandria, VA: ADA, 2011. 576 p.

15. American Diabetes Association. The diabetes comfort food cookbook. Alexandria, VA: ADA, 2011. 192 p.

16. American Diabetes Association. Ideas for exercise. American Diabetes Association [article online] 2012. Available from http://www.diabetes.org/food-and-fitness/fitness/ideas-for-exercise/?loc=DropDownFF-exerciseideas. Accessed 2012 Feb 22.

14

Creating Electronic Research Projects

Clear Targets

Electronic sources are now a major source of research information as well as a key component for the presentation of investigative analysis. To that end, this chapter suggests ways to create and publish your research project electronically.

- Developing electronic documents and slide shows
- Creating pages with Hypertext Markup Language (HTML)
- Using graphics in your electronic research paper
- Preparing a writing portfolio

Creating your research paper electronically has a number of advantages:

- *It is easy.* Creating electronic research papers can be as simple as saving a file, and your school probably has resources for publishing your paper electronically.
- *It offers multimedia potential.* Unlike paper documents, electronic documents enable you to include anything available in a digital form—including text, illustrations, sound, and video.
- *It can link your reader to more information.* Your reading can click a hyperlink to access additional sources of information. (A hyperlink or link is a highlighted word or image that, when clicked, lets readers jump from one place to another—for example, from your research paper to a website on your subject.)

14a Beginning the Electronic Project

Before you decide to create your research paper electronically, consider three questions to assist the development of the presentation:

1. **What support is provided by your school?** Investigate how your college will help you publish in an electronic medium.
2. **Is electronic publishing suitable for your research topic?** Ask yourself what your readers will gain from reading an electronic text rather than the traditional paper version.
3. **What form will it take?** Electronic research papers generally appear as an electronic presentation, a web page, or a printed document.

14b Building Electronic Presentations

If you plan an oral presentation, an electronic slide show can help illustrate your ideas. Commonly referred to as a PowerPoint presentation, the electronic presentation differs from word-processed documents in that each page, or slide, comprises one computer screen. By clicking, you can move to the next slide.

Because each slide can hold only limited information, condense the content of each slide.

14c Research Paper Web Pages and Sites

A website can be an exciting and flexible way to convey your research. It is also the easiest way to get your work out to a large audience. Like an electronic presentation, a research paper website can include graphics, sound, and video.

Creating a web page or a website involves collecting or making a series of computer files—some that contain the basic text and layout for your pages, and others that contain the graphics, sounds, or video that goes in your pages. These files are assembled together automatically when you view them in a web browser.

Creating a Web Page

The easiest way to create your pages is with a web page editor such as Microsoft FrontPage, Adobe Page Mill, or Netscape Composer. These programs work differently, but they all do the same thing—create web pages. Using them is like using a word processor: you enter or paste in text, insert graphics or other multimedia objects, and save the file.

The easiest but most limited method is to save your word-processed research paper in HTML (Hypertext Markup Language, the computer language that controls what websites look like). Different word-processing programs perform this process differently, so consult your software's help menu for specific instructions.

When the word-processing software converts your document to HTML, it also converts any graphics you have included to separate graphics files. Together, your text and the graphics can be viewed in a web browser like any other web page.

Your research paper will look somewhat different in HTML format than in its word-processed format. In some ways, HTML is less flexible than word processing, but you can still use word-processing software to make changes to your new HTML-formatted paper.

Citing Your Sources in a Web Research Paper

For a web research paper, include parenthetical citations in the text itself and create a separate web page for references. Remember to include hyperlinks that direct readers to the works cited in the paper.

14d Using Graphics in Your Electronic Research Paper

Graphics will give your electronic text some exciting features that are usually foreign to the traditional research paper. They go beyond

words on a printed page to pictures, sound, video clips, animation, and the vivid use of full-color art.

Decorative graphics make the document look more attractive but seldom add to the paper's content. Most clip art, for example, is decorative.

Pictures provide a visual amplification of the text. For example, a picture of Thomas Hardy would reinforce and augment a research paper on the British poet and novelist.

Information graphics, such as charts, graphs, or tables, provide data about your topic.

Graphics usually take up a lot of space, but you can save them as either JPEG or GIF files to make them smaller. In fact, websites can use only graphics saved in these formats. Both formats compress redundant information in a file, making it smaller while retaining most of the image quality. You can recognize the file format by looking at the extension to the file name—GIFs have the extension .gif, and JPEGs have the extension .jpg or .jpeg. GIF stands for Graphical Interchange Format, which develops and transfers digital images. JPEG stands for

Joint Photographic Experts Group, which compresses color images to smaller files for ease of transport.

In general, JPEGs work best for photographs and GIFs work best for line drawings. To save a file as a GIF or JPEG, open it in an image-editing program like Adobe Photoshop and save the file as one of the two types (for example, thardy.jpg or thardy.gif).

Creating Your Own Digital Graphics

Making your own graphics file is complex but rewarding. It adds a personal creativity to your research paper. Use one of the following techniques:

- **Use a graphics program**, such as Macromedia Freehand or Adobe Illustrator. With such software you can create a graphic file and save it as a JPEG or GIF.
- **Use a scanner** to copy your drawings, graphs, photographs, and other matter. Programs such as Adobe Photoshop and JASC Paintshop Pro are useful for modifying scanned photographs.
- **Create original photographs with a digital camera.** Digital cameras usually save images as JPEGs, so you will not need to convert the files into a usable format.

As long as you create JPEG files or GIF files for your graphics, you can transport the entire research paper to a website.

14e Delivering Your Electronic Research Paper to Readers

Follow your instructor's requirements for delivering your electronic research paper or use one of the techniques in the following checklist.

CHECKLIST

Delivering Your Electronic Research Paper

- **CD-ROM disks.** These disks hold large amounts of data and thus work well for transmitting graphics, sound, or video files. However, you must own or have access to a CD-R (Compact Disk Recordable) or CD-RW (Compact Disk Recordable/Writeable) drive. Most readers will have regular CD-ROM drives that can read your disks, but you might want to confirm this beforehand.

- **High-speed USB flash drive.** These devices hold large amounts of data, so they work well for transmitting graphics, sound, or video files. The compact size and plug and play operation allow easy access to your instructor's laptop or desktop computer with a USB port.

- **E-mail.** E-mailing your file as an attachment is the fastest way to deliver your electronic research paper; however, it works best if you have a single file, like a word-processed research paper, rather than a collection of related files, like a website.

- **Drop box.** Many schools are now utilizing online sharing folders. Students can select the class and subject online then submit their research paper to the teacher's "drop box." Check with your college for specific guidance and details of this submission process.

- **Website.** If you have created a website or web page, you can upload your work to a web server, and readers can access your work on the Internet. Procedures for uploading websites vary from school to school and server to server; work closely with your instructor and webmaster to perform this process successfully. Regardless of what method you choose, be sure to follow your instructor's directions and requirements.

14f   Preparing a Writing Portfolio

Over the past decade, writing portfolios have become a choice assessment tool for many instructors. The writing portfolio is a purposeful collection of writing assembled to demonstrate specified writing capabilities to an audience. Usually, a portfolio is used to demonstrate writing skills and talents, but it can also be used for obtaining a job, documenting job performance, or gaining entrance into an educational institution. In some respects, the writing portfolio is an individual's creative resume. Although it is not an actual resume, the writing portfolio displays the works and documents that a resume mentions. In that sense, the collection of writings gives a three-dimensional or amplified view of a learner's abilities.

Listed here are some criteria for selecting folio material:

- Select materials that clearly demonstrate your abilities.
- Select materials based on quality. Choose documents that demonstrate audience analysis, grammar, clarity, conciseness, technical information, instructions, page layout and design, organization, group or independent work, diversity, and variety.
- Select materials that demonstrate learning. For instance, if a particular piece demonstrates your understanding of persuasive methods, include it.

Note: The safest and most dependable way to store your materials is both as hard copy and on a flash drive.

APPENDIX
Glossary of
Manuscript Style

The alphabetical glossary that follows will answer most of your miscellaneous questions about matters of form, such as margins, pagination, dates, and numbers. For matters not addressed below, consult the index, which will direct you to appropriate pages elsewhere in this text.

Abbreviations

Employ abbreviations often and consistently in notes and citations, but avoid them in the text. In your citations, but not in your text, always abbreviate these items:

- Technical terms and reference words (anon., e.g., diss.)
- Institutions (acad., assn., Cong.)
- Dates (Jan., Feb.)
- States and countries (OH, CA, USA)
- Names of publishers (McGraw, UP of Florida)
- Titles of literary works (*Ado* for *Much Ado About Nothing*)
- Books of the Bible (Exod. for Exodus)

Accent Marks

When you quote, reproduce accents exactly as they appear in the original.

> "La tradición clásica en españa," according to Romana, remains strong in public school instruction (16).

Ampersand

Avoid using the ampersand symbol "&" unless custom demands it, as in the John Updike story title "A & P."

Arabic Numerals

Arabic numerals should be used whenever possible: for volumes, books, parts, and chapters of works; acts, scenes, and lines of plays; cantos, stanzas, and lines of poetry.

Figures and Tables

A table is a systematic presentation of materials, usually in columns. A figure is any nontext item that is not a table: blueprint, chart, diagram, drawing, graph, photo, photostat, map, and so on. Use graphs appropriately. A line graph serves a different purpose than a circle (pie) chart, and a bar graph plots different information than a scatter graph. Place captions above a table and below a figure. Here is an example:

Table 1: Response by Class on Nuclear Energy Policy

	Freshman	Sophomore	Junior	Senior
1. More nuclear power	150	301	75	120
2. Less nuclear power	195	137	111	203
3. Present policy is acceptable	87	104	229	31

Foreign Cities

In general, spell the names of foreign cities as they are written in original sources. However, for purposes of clarity, you may substitute an English name or provide both with one in parentheses:

Köln (Cologne)   Braunschweig (Brunswick)

Indention

Indent first lines of paragraphs five spaces or a half-inch. Indent all lines of long quotations (four lines or more) ten spaces or one inch from the left margin.

Italics

Use *italics* in place of <u>underscoring</u> for titles and words that require emphasis.

Margins

A basic one-inch margin on all sides is recommended. Place your page number one-half inch down from the top edge of the paper and one inch from the right edge. Your software will provide a ruler, menu, or style palette that allows you to set the margins. *Note:* If you develop a header, the running head may appear one inch from the top, in which case your first line of text will begin 1-1/2 inches from the top.

Names of Persons

As a general rule, the first mention of a person requires the full name (e.g., Ernest Hemingway or Margaret Mead) and thereafter give only the surname (e.g., Hemingway or Mead). *Note:* APA style uses last name only in the text. Omit formal titles (Mr., Mrs., Dr., Hon.) in textual and note references to distinguished persons, living or dead.

Numbering Pages

Use a running head to number your pages in the upper right-hand corner of the page. Depending on the software, you can create the head with the "numbering" or the "header" feature. See the sample paper for page numbers in MLA style, pages 150–154.

Roman Numerals

Use capital Roman numerals for titles of persons (Elizabeth II) and major sections of an outline (see pages 87–88). Use lowercase Roman numerals for preliminary pages of text, as for a preface or introduction (iii, iv, v). Otherwise, use Arabic numerals (e.g., Vol. 5, Act 2, Ch. 17, Plate 21, 2 Sam. 2.1–8, or *Iliad* 2.121–30), *except* when writing for some instructors in history, philosophy, religion, music, art, and theater, in which case you may need to use Roman numerals (e.g., III, Act II, I Sam. ii.1–8, *Hamlet* I.ii.5–6).

Running Heads

Repeat your last name in the upper-right corner of every page just in front of the page number (see the sample paper, pages 167–174).

Proofreading Marks

Be familiar with the most common proofreading symbols so that you can correct your own copy or mark your copy for a typist. Some of the most common proofreading symbols are shown below:

Common Proofreading Symbols

i	error in spelling (m*i*stake) with correction in margin
lc	lowercase (misTake)
⌒	close up (mis take)
I	delete and close up (misstake)
⊢⊣	delete and close up more than one letter (the mistakes and errors continue)
∧	insert (mi∧take)
∿ *tr*	transpose elements (thier)
⬯	material to be corrected or moved, with instructions in the margin, or material to be spelled out ((corp))
caps or ≡	capitalize (Huck finn and Tom Sawyer)
¶	begin a paragraph
No¶	do not begin a paragraph
∧	insert
℮	delete (a mistakes)
#	add space
⊙	add a period
∧	add a comma
∧	add a semicolon
∨	add an apostrophe or single closing quotation mark
∨	add a single opening quotation mark
∨ ∨	add double quotation marks
bf	change to boldface
ital	change to italic
stet	let stand as it is; ignore marks
� or (I)	add parentheses
=	add a hyphen

Shortened Titles in the Text

Use abbreviated titles of books and articles mentioned often in the text after a first, full reference. For example, after initial usage, *Backgrounds to English as Language* should be shortened to *Backgrounds* in the text, notes, and in-text citations.

Spacing

As a general rule, double-space everything—the body of the paper, all indented (block) quotations, and all reference entries. Footnotes, if used, should be single-spaced, but endnotes should be double-spaced (see pages 181–182). APA style (see Chapter 11) requires double-spacing after all headings and to separate text from indented quotes and figures.

Titles Within Titles

For the title of an article within quotation marks that includes a title to a book, retain the use of italics.

> "*Great Expectations* as a Novel of Initiation"

For a title of an article within quotation marks that includes another title indicated by quotation marks, enclose the shorter title within single quotation marks.

> "A Reading of O. Henry's 'The Gift of the Magi'"

For the title to a book that incorporates another title that is normally italicized, do not italicize the shorter title nor place it within quotation marks.

> *Interpretations of* Great Expectations
> *Using Shakespeare's* Romeo and Juliet *in the Classroom*

Word Division

Avoid dividing any word at the end of a line. Leave the line short rather than divide a word.

Credits

Index